Falling

This book is great for couples that are tired of the fighting and are ready to repair the relationship. If people took the time to understand relationships and follow the recommendations as explained in your book, there would be less divorce and more long lasting marriages. The book was easy to read, understand and very informative. I did not want to put down. It is definitely worth reading more than once. I would recommend your book to anyone who has love for another person.

— **CURTIS MCNAUGHT,** Bloomfield Hills, MI

I have been married for fifteen years and thought it was a "perfect" marriage. This book is the key to what we've been missing. I have become much closer to my husband because of it. This book is the best gift to give to your friends of family members. They will love you for it!!

— **TINA BATEMAN,** Insurance Agent, Brighton, MI.

Falling in love is the easy part. Staying in love takes work. Learn a new approach to understanding your partner's needs. Know how to be there for each other and become Best Friends, as well as lovers.

— **ANNETTE MEYER RUFF,** MS, Brighton, MI

Falling in Love is Not Enough *describes the type of relationship we all hope for - past the rush of "falling in love" to the deeper, more satisfying "safe haven" relationships. This book gives me the understanding I need to create my own great relationship. It will do the same for you.*

— **ANN SAVICKAS,** BSW, JD, Attorney, Ann Arbor

If you are looking for a new way to improve your relationship, one that works, this is the book for you. It is loaded with great insight to help you become happier and closer with your partner. It reads easily and gives ideas in an easily understood way. It should be taught in high school. I wish I had this knowledge long ago.

— **LINDA NICHOLS,** Account Executive, Lansing, MI

falling in love
is not enough

Keeping Your Love
Alive Forever

falling in love
is not enough

Keeping Your
Love Alive Forever

Joseph Dragun, Ph.D.

Canton Press
Brighton, MI

Falling In Love Is Not Enough
Keeping Your Love Alive Forever

Joseph Dragun, Ph.D.

Canton Press
P.O. Box 1047, Brighton, MI 48116-1047
(810) 229-9192, fax (810) 227-6982
e-mail: cantonpress@sbcglobal.net

Book and cover design by:
Peri Poloni-Gabriel, Knockout Design, www.knockoutbooks.com

Manufactured in the United States of America on acid-free paper.

Publisher's Cataloging-In-Publication Data
(prepared by Quality Books)

Dragun, Joseph.
    Falling in love is not enough : keeping your love
alive forever / Joseph Dragun.
        p. cm.
    Includes bibliographical references.
    LCCN 2006921130
    ISBN-13: 978-0-9763799-3-5
    ISBN-10: 0-9763799-3-7

    1. Marital psychotherapy—Popular works.
    2. Attachment behavior—Popular works. 3. Love.
    4. Man-woman relationships. I. Title.

RC488.5.D73 2006   616.89'1562
        QBI06-600045

contents

the author

Joseph Dragun is a licensed clinical psychologist with extensive experience in therapy. Prior to becoming a counselor, he administered several not-for-profit human service organizations. His practice focuses upon helping to improve relationships between couples, children and parents, peers, and supervisors and employees. He is certified in Emotionally Focused Therapy for Couples and he trains and supervises other therapists in this exciting and highly effective method of treatment. He has given numerous presentations on a variety of topics.

Visits Dr. Dragun's website at

www.keepinglove.com.

acknowledgements

T here are many people whom I wish to acknowledge. Gail Palmer gave me valuable insight into the practical application of this treatment. Susan Johnson developed the method of Emotionally Focused Therapy for Couples, on which this book is based. I also thank the couples who have taught me to be a better therapist.

This book was also shaped by several people who have read the manuscript and have given me valuable feedback. These include Tina Bateman; Alfred Dodini, Ph.D., director of the Anasazi Institute; Annette Meyers; Curtis McNaught; Susan Nestler, Ph.D., a talented therapist in Philadelphia; Linda Nichols; Ann Savickas; Diane Sollee, MSW, founder and director of the Coalition for Marriage, Family and Couples Education and the director of the annual Smart Marriages conference; my colleague Anne Solomon, LMSW; and Gary L. Thomas, writer and director of the Center for Evangelical Spirituality.

My thanks and deep gratitude to all my friends, colleagues, and loved ones. They generously offered their encouragement and patiently listened whenever I had writers block and panicked.

introduction

No one marries hoping to divorce. Few become involved in intimate relationships with the expectation of breaking up. Yet couples frequently split up even after giving their best efforts to stay together.

I have studied and tried different types of couple's therapy. All offer some guidance, but most seem to miss the boat. The therapies don't help most people repair their relationships in a lasting way, and the studies bear this out. Most marriage therapies have only a thirty-five percent success rate, and the rate of relapse is great. This means that despite initial improvement couples tend to fall back into their old patterns of unhappiness. Most therapies misfire because they do not effectively deal with the essential and central issues we face in relationships.

This book describes what makes relationships last. It's about two kinds of love: short-term "falling-in-love" and long-term "attachment love."

Most Westerners marry because they have fallen-in-love. This book will show you how we make mistakes when we rely solely on this kind of love. Much more is necessary for a marriage, or any intimate relationship, to succeed. Becoming skilled in the art of long-term "attachment love" produces a more lasting relationship. Falling-in-love is not enough.

It will become clear to you how well-intentioned people fail while others succeed. As you read on, the absolute essentials of successful relationships will become clear. You will be introduced to the common sense principles of attachment love and see how this love plays out in relationships. You will discover how our hot buttons can distort our love, and finally you will learn concrete ways to improve your relationship.

These ideas are based upon a very effective kind of couples counseling. This therapy, *Emotionally Focused Therapy for Couples* (EFT), developed by Dr. Susan Johnson, has been proven to help 90% of couples. And it's long-lasting. Two years after therapy, 75% of couples report they still are happy with each other.

A word of warning. It's not easy to change old patterns. Although some books imply otherwise, there's no magic pill that automatically makes it all better. Yet with work, effort, and commitment you can improve your relationship.

the mystery of love

Talk to one hundred different people about love. You will find that they can give you anecdotes, stories and examples. But if you ask those same people to define love in such a way that it can apply to all of those cases, you will receive numerous definitions. They join the legion of poets, writers, psychologists, sociologists and philosophers who have tried their hand at defining this elusive phenomenon.

These writers have both areas of agreement and differences. I suspect that the reason for this is simple. Love is a mystery. Like life itself, it is bigger than any of us. The best that anyone can do is to describe it from one's own point of view.

This book can help you keep your love for your partner alive and well. The viewpoint, assumptions and biases are from the discipline of psychology. Loving relationships of all kinds are defined in terms of attachment theory. Thus we use the term, attachment love, to describe the bond between intimate partners.

But it is only one point of view (though I think it is a pretty good one). After all, love is larger than psychology. This chapter presents some important ideas, from other perspectives, about the nature of love. I include them because clients repeat these themes over and over again in our sessions. Even more importantly, I find that these descriptions have the ring of truth to them. They help describe my understanding of the mystery of love.

An Emotional Response

Love involves several aspects of being a human being, including knowledge, attention, perception, fantasy and emotions. Knowledge involves knowing something about the person. One must focus attention upon the person in order to see or perceive something about them. Fantasies are involved. For example, people dream about a possible future with a person. In order to live and love, we use these various aspects of our personalities. So it is not very helpful to spend a lot of time talking about them. But emotions are different. A major theme among writers is that the core of love is an emotional or affective response of some kind.

Desire and Care

One such response is desire. Love often leads to a desire for something for the beloved. This is easy to see. If I love my children, I may want them to do well in school so that they may get a better job. In the same vein, this desire prompts people to give things to their beloved. Children are provided a home, food and the things they need to grow. Lovers financially support their partners. Needed things are generously provided.

Lovers give of themselves in other ways. They give wisdom, advice, time, support, teaching and other qualities which they possess and which the beloved needs. Often gifts are given even though the beloved does not need them. Presents, whether simple or extravagant, are given to show the deep love a person has for another.

This desire to give appears to be a strong part of love. But the foundation for this desire is "care". It simply makes no sense to give things to a person you don't care about. Conversely, the more one cares about someone, the more one desires to give, even if there is no need. Part of the reality of love involves caring and taking responsibility for the beloved. It is caring for the beloved whether or not something is needed.

But care is also given in many situations when one is not in love. A nurse may care for and desire that a patient improve, even while love is not present. I care about U.S. soldiers abroad and desire that they return home. I do not love them. Desire and care are a part of love. But since they also exist independently of love, I believe that they are not the essence or center of love. We have to look further to find the essence of love.

Affection and Joy

Though most writers agree that emotions are a central part of love, they have many conflicting opinions. Some go so far to equate love with joy. One writer describes love as a subtle feeling, of delight or satisfaction when in the presence of a love one, even when anxiety or anger is present.

I have a hard time with this position. Certainly I feel happiness and affection for my beloved. But not always. Sometimes I am sad, hurt or angry with her. Yet I still love her. My children, at times, have exasperated me. Yet I still love them. So how can I say that affection and joy are the center of love? It is not always there.

Besides, if happiness were the center of love, how can I explain the fact that I can feel happiness for people who I clearly do not love. I am happy when my team wins. But I do not love the Detroit Pistons.

Part of the confusion stems from how we use the term "love." When a person likes or enjoys something, they often say, "I love it." I love eating lasagna made in the Bolognese style. What I am really saying is that I enjoy or like it. But is this the same kind of love as I have for my daughter? Similarly, some people really enjoy being with someone else and sometimes confuse this with love.

None of these emotions are the essence of love, even though they are felt while in love. Emotions are powerfully affected by love, but they are not the same.

Union

Many couples sense some sort of union with each other. In some way they feel that they have become "one" with each other. Erich Fromm made popular the idea that love is a union. In a way this makes a lot of sense. People genetically have a fundamental need for union with someone or something. The attachment theory of love begins at this point: we have an innate need to be bonded with someone. Attachment love involves a safe bonding or union with the beloved. Many people who have fallen-in-love can describe the intense desire to be completely and totally unified with the beloved.

A union of some kind with the beloved seems to be a part of love. But what is the nature of this union? How can it be defined and described?

Union is really a kind of "presence". Presence is co-existing with another person. It is "being with" someone or something else. There are different dimensions to presence. On one level, one can be physically present with someone or something. I am physically present with a man if I am in the same room with him, whether I notice this person or not.

Another level is cognitive presence. This is an intellectual awareness of something. I am not only in the room with someone, I focus my attention on them, find out their name and know what they do for a living. There are degrees of depth to this type of presence. One may have a passing knowledge of a new acquaintance. Or one may have quite a bit of information about a good friend. But in both instances, there is a cognitive presence.

A yet deeper dimension is affective, or emotional, presence. This means that you have some feelings for a person or thing. People "love" cars, art, cooking, fishing, money, deer hunting, backpacking, golfing, music and/or any number of things. You like the object or occupation. Or you may hate it. Both are examples of affective presence.

It is the same with people. I may dislike my boss or love her. But because I have some emotions for her, I have affective presence with her. Some may think that anger or hatred is the opposite of emotional presence. But these are also emotions. The opposite of affective presence is actually indifference, the lack of any emotion. An emotion is felt only if you have some level of affective presence.

Union in love may involve all three levels of presence. It certainly involves cognitive presence and emotional presence. Physical presence is not necessarily needed. You can love someone who is currently half-way around the world in a war zone. But it is hard to see how one can love someone without being emotionally and cognitively present.

Though union and presence are in love, more is needed. After all, one can have an emotional response to modern art (by hating it) and not be in love with it. It seems to me that a special kind of emotional presence is involved in love.

You in Me

Union in love has a quality which appears unique and special. Lovers talk about being "one" with each other. It is as if each lived in the other.

Jules Toner was a philosopher who studied the experience of love. He believed that a harmony exists between lovers. This accord is based neither on shared beliefs, interests, opinions nor activities. Love itself creates something new. Each senses and shares the other's life on some basic, emotional level. The lover feels as if the beloved's life is his or her life. The beloved's life becomes the lover's life.

Here is another way to describe it. When in love, I am in union and am present with my loved one, so much so that I feel as if her life is mine. I am aware of my own life and, in addition, I live my beloved's life as if it were my own.

At first glance, this may seem far-fetched. Yet common, everyday examples point to this reality. Consider a child and its parent. The child has a part in winning a soccer game and is happy. The parent is happy for the child, because the child has succeeded. This parent is not thinking of him or herself. Nor is there any thought of reflected glory, such as thinking how great a parent they are because of "my" child's success. The parent is merely aware of the child's happiness and success and experiences it as if it were their own success.

Think of a time when your child was hurt and was in pain. Did you not feel the pain, as if it were your own? I vividly remember an incident involving my son, who was about six at the time. He got his finger pinched in a shopping mall door. I felt fear, even sickness, as I extracted him from the door and took him for treatment. It was as if the injury had occurred to me. I seemed to live through the event just as he did.

A few months before my father died, he lost his ability to walk and became depressed and withdrawn. I was constantly aware of his pain and sadness as I tried to interact with him. It was as if his pain was my own. In fact, it became exceedingly difficult for me to tolerate those feelings.

When working with couples, one partner will express their sadness and hurt regarding some incident. Sometimes this incident involves their partner, sometimes not. I then ask the other partner to share his or her reaction. If union and care for the other are present, this partner will say they are sad, bothered, upset, hurt or disturbed by their partner's revelation.

In intimate loving relationships, one partner reacts when their partner is upset. Often, couples tell me that when their partner comes home upset, they are bothered by it and react to it. They feel their partner's pain as if it were their own pain. In fact they are in pain. The lover is one with the beloved. The beloved is present in the lover's life. The lover responds to the beloved's life as if it were their own life.

Union is Not Submission, Domination or Imitation

This union in love is not about one person submerging or losing oneself in another person. It is not about someone dominating their beloved. It is true that some need to control in order to feel safe. Fear of abandonment sometimes is countered with attempts to control and dominate one's partner. But this is not the essence of the union which love creates.

Nor is it about a conformity in which both think, act and emote the same exact way. Some couples do create a kind of unanimity. They have highly similar opinions, goals, points of view and interests. Maybe they even dress alike. They possess a kind of harmony in their lives based on these similarities. Yet there are many loving couples who have very dissimilar interests and who even belong to different political parties. So love does not arise out of this attitudinal unity or any kind of conformity. It is an act of union by which your beloved's reality as a person is felt as if it were your own. Out of this harmony and union, couples sometimes find that their opinions and interests begin to converge. The union of love comes first.

Union in love is not about identifying with and imitating the beloved. People sometimes search out gurus and heroes. Kids often look for and imitate a superhero. Children feel weak and small. But if they can identify with a Superman, they can fantasize and become stronger, at least in their imagination. Adults may look for a teacher, a mentor, a beloved to identify with and imitate. Their own weakness can then be countered and offset by the greater strength of their hero. Even adults sometimes identify with another out of fear or jealousy. But union in love does not involve this process. In union, the lover sees and knows their own weaknesses and the weaknesses of the beloved. Both lives are embraced and experienced as the lover's own.

Parents have been known to try to live their lives through their children. A father encourages a son to play football so that the father can re-live his own glory days. Someone might want their child to "follow in his footsteps" at work as a way of perpetuating his or her dynasty and glory. At those moments, the union of love is not present. This father focuses on his own emotional and psychological gain. He uses his son to feel better about himself.

The union of love involves sensing that the beloved is part of you, while fully knowing that your beloved is a different person.

So a father feels happy when his son succeeds. This same father also knows that it is his son's life. Not his life. A woman feels the pain her husband feels when he has not succeeded at work, as if it were his own pain. Yet she knows that it is his life, not hers.

Real love, between two people, is an act of union in which each somehow wants to be in the beloved and wants the beloved to be in them. There is no loss of either self. It is a kind of welcoming of the beloved in to one's world and self. It is making a harmony with the beloved being and life. It is feeling and reacting to the beloved's life, as if it were your own. It is an emotional union with the beloved.

Giving of Self

I have heard men say that their financially supporting their family is their expression of their love. Lovers give each other gifts because it is an integral part of love. But in the light of the above, it takes on a different, deeper character. The clue comes in Janis' reactions.

Kerry had purchased a quadrunner for Janis, his wife. He proudly presented it to her. She took one look at it, starting thinking of its cost and of their credit card debt, and coldly asked him if he was out of his mind. Kerry was deeply hurt and offended by Janis' statements. They got into a terrible argument. I remember purchasing a vacuum cleaner for my wife, who told me to take this Christmas present back. I know how Kerry felt.

Yes, he probably should have talked to Janis about it. Yes, I should have gotten something more personal for my wife for a Christmas gift. But we both felt terribly hurt because we were rejected. On some level the gift was an expression of us. When the gifts were rejected, if is as if we were rejected.

I am happy to say that we both got over our trauma. But we both learned much about love. We don't just give money or time or advice. We don't just give of some quality which we own. The giving is not just a symbol for one's love. We don't give "of ourselves." In love we give ourselves. Even as one takes in the beloved into one's personal life and emotions, we hope the beloved will take us in. We are the gift.

Accepting

The equation of giving demands an acceptance. One simply can't occur without the other. This is an important aspect of love. Often therapists hear that one partner does not accept the other. What does this mean?

The term usually refers to one's attitude and intention towards a person or a situation. According to the Oxford English Dictionary, it comes from a Latin word which means "to receive what is offered" and "to take in." It defines the word in four basic ways:

- To receive willingly or with consent
- To undertake as a responsibility
- To receive with favor
- To receive as sufficient

In the union created in love, I accept my partner in such a way that she is emotionally present in me. I "take in" my beloved in my emotional make-up. But this "taking in" does not involve the qualities, characteristics, opinions and interests which the loved one might possess. It is not about accepting these characteristics. Somehow you receive internally your beloved as a personal being and make this person an emotional part of your life.

The first definition above involves consent. The loved one is received willingly. There is no coercion, no force. You enter into the relationship freely.

The second meaning can be related to giving and caring. By accepting the loved one into your life, you also accept responsibility for the loved one's presence in your life. Sometimes the acceptance demands a response of working for what the loved one needs. One may be called to problem solve and give of your time. It may involve responding emotionally and sharing your reactions to events which occur in your beloved's life. Perhaps giving comfort is needed. It may involve simply watching your grandchild while he explores a meadow of grass and wildflowers.

The third and fourth descriptions above have powerful psychological meanings, at least for me. One receives the beloved with favor. How do you receive someone with favor into your home? You welcome them with happiness, try to make them comfortable, get them any food or drink they might want or need, introduce them to people they might not know and maybe show them around the place. You let them know that you appreciate them with your words and with your actions. Similarly in the union of love, one accepts the beloved, showing and telling them that you approve of them on a basic, personal level.

Part of the acceptance also involves your attitudes regarding the basic value and worthiness of your beloved. Is your loved one valuable, important, worthy or not? Is your beloved sufficient or not? In the emotional union of love, your loved one is valued as an important person. This is not to be confused with faults, weaknesses and lack of knowledge.

Let me give you an example. I tried to repair a wall in my home. I worked hard, but the wall looked lousy when I finally quit. I failed. This is a reflection of my lack of knowledge and skill. It does not say anything about my value and worth as a person. It simply means I should hire a carpenter the next time around. Similarly, in the acceptance of love, one's partner is viewed as sufficient, worthy and valuable, even though you might be painfully aware of his or her weaknesses.

As Thomas Gordon, a clinical psychologist, points out, parental acceptance significantly affects children. Many parents have been brought up to believe that if you accept children they will remain just the way they are. So the best way to help children improve is to tell them what you don't accept about them. These parents rely heavily on the language of unacceptance in rearing children, believing this is the best way to help them. They evaluate, judge, criticize, preach, moralize, admonish, command and punish. For children, as well as adults, these messages convey unacceptance. These parents love their children deeply, but mistakenly emphasize language and communication which negates that love.

When a person knows that he or she is genuinely accepted by another, that person can more easily grow, develop, make constructive changes, learn to solve problems, and become more productive and creative. This is a paradox of love. When your loved one feels truly accepted by you in the union of love, his or her life becomes easier and happier.

Love

In this chapter I have tried to give you my perspective on the essence of love. Like life, love is ultimately a mystery which defies complete, scientific definition. But some themes can be identified. These appear again and again in the rest of this book. Love involves:

- A union between two people.
- In the union the lover takes in another person in such a way that their life is emotionally lived as if it were their own.
- In response to the beloved, one feels affection and joy, as well as pain, hurt, sorrow and every other emotion which exists.
- It involves caring, both emotionally and physically.
- Giving of oneself is central.
- The lover accepts the beloved.

The next chapter explores the wonderful feeling of falling-in-love and how people go about finding their beloved.

Hark close and still what I now whisper to you
I love you, O you entirely possess me,

O that you and I escape from the rest, and go utterly off,
free and lawless,

Two hawks in the air, two fishes swimming in the sea
not more lawless than we;

That furious storm through me careening.
I passionately trembling;

The oath of the inseparableness of two together,
Of the woman that loves me, and whom I love
More than my life, that oath swearing,
O I willingly stake all for you…

WALT WHITMAN
"From Pent-up Aching Rivers"

Chapter 2

a fantastic experience

⌐⦙⌐

"Falling in love" is a most exhilarating experience. Ah, to fall in love. The intensity of the relationship! All else pales by comparison. I love Gene Kelly in "Singing in the Rain." As Gene dances in the street, oblivious to the rain, he captures for us that glorious feeling — an irreplaceable high. I suspect that a part of each one of us secretly hopes to recapture and live that high.

Jim, my client, told me how every moment is so sweet. He couldn't get enough of his partner. He wanted to spend all of his time with her. Whether at work or school, his thoughts strayed to her. Time seemed to stand still as he impatiently waited for the moment he would see her again. In contrast, all of his other activities and endeavors seemed pale, drab and meaningless. He even created a kind of fantasy around this woman. How wonderful it would be to be together with her. To have children. To live together for all time. To grow old together, and even to die together.

She was his dream woman. His dream mate. Or to invoke a more current metaphor — his "soul mate." She would make up for all the things that were wrong with him. She would make his life greater than anything he'd ever experienced before. All of his problems would be solved. He would be happy, gloriously happy, for the rest of his life living with the perfect woman of his dreams.

Then Jim told me the rest of his story. He and his beloved got married and had a few kids. After a few years, like so many other couples they began to fight. Despite his work and best efforts, he and his wife — the woman he once so desperately loved — divorced. Jim was devastated and could not understand how this happened. How could two people who had been so gloriously in love end up hating each other? Obviously, falling-in-love is not enough.

What is this celebrated condition all about? Why do people experience it? Where does it come from? How do people get it? How long does it last? Why does it end? This and the next chapter describe falling-in-love, and the problems it can create.

Genetically Programmed

Falling-in-love has been around for as long as people have existed. Literature and poetry from different cultures and ages describe this phenomenon. It can even be found in the Old Testament. The "Song of Solomon" appears to describe the ecstasy of falling-in-love. (In fairness to other commentators, it's also interpreted as God's love for his people). It's not difficult to accept that falling-in-love is a timeless, universal human happening; and an extraordinarily sweet one at that. Different cultures do not always have the same attitudes about it as Westerners, but more on that later.

Where does falling-in-love come from? Some anthropologists believe that we are genetically programmed for it. The purpose is simple: to raise children. People are first sexually attracted to each other. Then falling-in-love may kick in. In this stage, a person focuses exclusively on a single possible mate. We are then driven to form an exclusive, intense bond with a prospective partner. The result is a union or a marriage. In such a relationship children can be born and raised to adulthood.

No wonder we have fantasies about marrying or living with our beloved. This is the way it's supposed to work. We are programmed for falling-in-love.

I am sure you can think of exceptions. Different people and cultures have other understandings and expectations. For example, in our culture people beyond child-bearing age experience falling-in-love. They do not want more children, yet they choose to bond. It appears to be a genetic component of our make up; we are hard-wired for it.

How We Fall-in-Love

Though commonly acknowledged that "love is blind," researchers have discovered many obvious characteristics. For example, they note that people tend to fall for others who are *physically near them*. It only makes sense that it would be difficult to be involved with someone we have never met (though it does happen, for example, through letters and the internet). But in general, people fall-in-love with people who are nearby.

The probability of such a relationship blossoming also increases when we see the person frequently. Since the likelihood of seeing each other and meeting is great, people tend to fall-in-love with those who live near them, work with them, or play with them.

Physical Appearance and Beauty

Another characteristic is the *physical appearance* of your prospective romantic partner. We are not attracted to people we consider unattractive. Sometimes we do get to know them and begin to see and appreciate other qualities; however, for many people, at least initially, physical attractiveness is an important factor in the falling-in-love process. This is equally true for both men and women.

If you don't believe this, just observe the dating services. They always include (or ask for) a picture or a videotape of the person looking for a partner. People want to see what their prospective partners look like. Most of us compare our physical traits and beauty with others, and the romantic partner one chooses tends to show a similar level of attractiveness. Of course, this is a highly subjective process. Beauty is in the eye of the beholder. Yet we tend to seek out those people whom we believe have a similar level of beauty.

Our tendency to judge people by appearance is an unfortunate aspect of being human, yet a factor nevertheless. People, in general, desire to be around attractive people and beautiful surroundings. But remember, studies show that attractive people possess no more positive traits or skills or abilities than those regarded as less attractive people.

Character

This is also a factor in how people choose. Men tend to seek partners who are sweet, smart, energetic, self-confidant, and easy-to-talk-to. Women look for men who are easy-going and intelligent. Both sexes desire prospective partners who are funny, sensitive, and warm.

Similarities

We tend to be attracted to others who show a similarity in interests, values, levels of physical beauty, attitudes, levels of intelligence and the same degree of psychological health. We also tend to be attracted to people who have a similar cultural background. There is even evidence to suggest that people are attracted to others who are genetically similar.

People tend to fall-in-love with others who come from the same class in society. In short, not too many blue-collar auto-workers end up marrying blue-bloods or Boston Brahmins or the Prince of Wales.

Loving the One Who Loves You

We have a tendency to fall-in-love with someone who is attracted to us. When people meet and are attracted to each other, a positive feedback loop is started. One person's attraction and attention kindles feelings of attraction in the other; this in turn precipitates an even greater reaction in the first person.

If you treat someone as if he or she were sexy and exciting, this person will very possibly become so and treat you the same way. Such is the essence of reciprocity in attraction: we are, clearly, attracted to others who are attracted to us. We pay attention to those who pay attention to us.

Emotional Arousal

One of the strongest, most powerful precursors to falling-in-love is *emotional arousal*. Simply put, we have a tendency to fall-in-love when we are emotionally aroused. Such an arousal can be either painful or joyful. We can be happy because of a promotion or sad because someone in our family has died. Either one is an emotional arousal which makes it more likely that a person will fall-in-love.

This emotional arousal is not merely the happy feeling one might have at the end of a day. It's a more intense feeling and state of being that stays with the person for a period of time.

Imagine how you might feel if you were fired. Or remember how you felt when your first boyfriend or girlfriend dumped you. These are the intense feelings that seem to consume us and preoccupy us for a length of time. These states prime us for falling-in-love.

It may sound strange and complicated, but it makes sense. During the Viet Nam war my good friend came back from boot camp just prior to being shipped off to Nam. In a few days he fell passionately in love with a mutual friend to whom he had never previously been attracted. After returning from the war, even he could not understand what happened. Now it's clear that his aroused emotions made him a prime candidate. He felt very sad and lonely about being away from home and extremely anxious about going into a war, and these intense emotions primed him to fall-in-love.

After a divorce people feel lonely, unloved, sad, and anxious about the future. They are vulnerable to falling-in-love on a rebound. Counselors recommend that after a divorce people should not even date for a year or two, during which time their aroused emotions typically make them vulnerable.

There are stories of hostages who fall in love with their captors. This "Stockholm Syndrome" may very well have its roots in the heightened emotional arousal of the captives. Romances are also started during exciting or unusual vacations.

One researcher describes the phenomenon of folk-dancing love. People who dance four and five days a week are physically and emotionally aroused by the dancing. This activity has a tendency to arouse and reinforce positive feelings for one's partner. At times, one may fall madly in love with his or her partner. Emotional arousal, of any kind, can set us up for falling-in-love.

Cultural Beliefs and Expectations

Our culture emphasizes falling-in-love. We've all heard such expressions as "love at first sight," "made for each other," and "soul mate." These phrases help generate the excitement and anticipation that we should and will fall-in-love. Some believe that such love is the only answer to human existence and the pursuit of happiness.

"The Notebook," a film released in the summer of 2004, starts out with an old man reading from a faded old notebook to an old woman. The pages include the story of her life. She has Alzheimer's disease and can't remember much of the past, but the old man reads to her as a reminder. The pages magically come alive with her life story.

In her past she had fallen-in love with a boy in her small hometown, and the boy had also fallen-in-love with her. However, her parents disapproved and took her away to another town. Several years later, he sees her and her fiancé. She goes back to visit him at the old hometown and their love is rekindled. She eventually chooses to marry "the love of her life" and they live happily ever after.

Movie after movie emphasizes and celebrates "falling in love." So many movies have this theme that the list alone could fill a large book. Hollywood makes this a major theme. But remember, Hollywood only gives us what we find attractive. Thus we grow up with the expectation and hope that we will fall in love, that it will lead to marriage and that this intense feeling will last forever.

We certainly believed it to be a simple, straight-forward process: you fall-in-love; you marry; you live happily ever after. Only it doesn't last and it's replaced by something different. Men and women make decisions based on faulty information about how love works. They make flawed decisions, not realizing that "attachment love" is every bit as important, if not more so, than falling-in-love. And this kind of love is more lasting, but more on this later.

Other Cultures

For many cultures, falling-in-love is not the basis of marriage. In various parts of the world the marriages of sons and daughters are still arranged by families. They have been arranged for reasons of state and power (e.g., kings arranged marriages for political reasons), and to obtain financial security and a stable economic situation for the family or for the anticipated newborn grandchild.

In India, marital love is considered the center of life. Men and women *expect* to fall in love with their arranged spouse. Even though this appears backward to Westerners, it happens often. Actually it's only in the relatively recent past that falling-in-love has become the main reason for getting married. Part of the reason people fall-in-love is that they expect it to happen.

Stages of Falling-In-Love

There are various theories that seek to explain the stages of falling-in-love and marrying. Some describe two, three, four or more different stages of the process, which occur in a definite order. Other theories describe a gradual process.

The following makes the most sense to me. It begins with our expectation that we want to experience falling-in-love. Then people meet others in their geographic area, which defines the pool of potential partners. We begin screening these people using the various standards listed above. When we are emotionally aroused, we fall-in-love with that lucky guy or gal. If all is in order, we form a relationship and expect to live happily ever after.

In theory, it sounds great. But this tells only one part of the story. First, couples, blinded by their intense emotions, make mistakes in evaluating their partners. Second, it invariably ends. If you expect it to last forever, your expectations of being happy will soon dissolve.

The next chapter looks at the trials and tribulations of falling-in-love.

love as addiction

~~⟨⟩~~

Falling-in-love is often not as reasonable and intellectual as one might infer from the previous chapter. Once we "fall" into it, a variety of things can happen. In fact, things can get really crazy and lead to problems. It has some great highs but it also has a dark side.

The Honeymoon Ends

One day it simply stopped. Or maybe it gradually faded away. My parents have referred to that moment as "the day the honeymoon ended." It was the day I woke up and asked myself: What did I get into? I am married, for life. Yeah, the party was great. But now I have this wife who ignores me, who doesn't want sex every night, who has these irritating habits, who says I am selfish, who seems to get angry for no reason, and who is not at all like the woman I fell in love with.

I know that women go through the same thing, because they have told me so. They wake up and find a husband who complains that the house is not clean enough, who reminds them that the chores are not done, who has a hissyfit if he doesn't get sex when he wants it, and who seems to disappear whenever the subject of "feelings" comes up.

Falling-in-love is often involuntary. Indeed, people typically just "fall" into it. Almost sixty percent of men and women believe that they had "no choice." It just happened to them. They neither planned for it nor arranged it nor intellectually chose to be in love. So what happened? Believe it or not, it can be a kind of addiction.

An Addiction?

If you look at addictions, the resemblance to falling-in-love is uncanny. In addictions, people spend much time thinking about their drug of choice. Often considerable time is spent procuring this drug and using it. And once the use begins, it becomes an involuntary and uncontrollable process.

Addicts become psychologically dependent upon their addictive behavior. The vast majority of drugs can be physiologically kicked in a few days. However, the psychological dependence is much more powerful and difficult to break.

Users literally and truly feel that they can't live without it. Once they start using a drug, often it is impossible to stop. They believe that they have almost no choice in the matter but to continue using their drug.

Efficiency at work is lost through drug use and during the recovery from the after-effects. As the behavior takes over more and more of one's life, the user becomes preoccupied with its use. The addictive behavior becomes central to one's world.

Users are said to be "in denial." They notice their drug use yet ignore how it affects their lives and the lives of their families. It becomes easy to deny even how much of the drug is taken. For people who are addicted, reality becomes distorted.

Falling in love

Believe it or not, falling-in-love matches this description of addiction. Attention is focused on the beloved. There is a preoccupation with the object of love, and one can't help but think about one's beloved. Thus work and school or other things suffer.

The lovers experience a roller-coaster ride of emotions. Each feels intense joy when the beloved is near and great sadness when the two are apart. The lovers feel insecurity and jealousy when their partner ignores them in the slightest way.

Life is restructured around the beloved, since a great amount of time and energy is spent with the beloved. It's often experienced as involuntary and uncontrollable. After having fallen-in-love, one frequently believes that he or she can't live life without the beloved. Each wants to be "one" with the other. Each can't get enough of his or her beloved. Each is inexorably drawn like a moth to the flame.

There is blindness in falling-in-love. Lovers do seem to notice each other's fault or faults, yet the meaning is distorted; the lover sees his beloved as wonderful beyond anything imaginable. Faults are merely unique, charming aspects of the other's personality. Differences are ignored. Reality is distorted. Clearly falling-in-love does suggest similarities to an addictive process.

Evidence Found in Brain Chemistry

Researchers have found that the brain reacts in a unique pattern when a person is fallen-in-love. Most of these differences involve what are called "neurotransmitters."

Our brains are composed of ten billion neurons which fire electrical impulses. The impulse starts at one end of the cell and moves to the opposite end. Each neuron in the brain makes contact with about one thousand other neurons, and each neuron stimulates these adjacent neurons to fire an electrical charge. It does this by shooting off chemicals in the small space, a synapse, where the two cells meet. The chemicals are called — guess what? — "neurotransmitters." These chemicals hit the adjacent neurons and fire them. In this way, electrical impulses travel through the body and in the brain. The neurotransmitters are important in psychology because different levels of them are associated with certain emotional and motivational states of the person.

Scientists have conducted studies seeking to determine which parts of the brain are activated by falling-in-love. They took students who said they had fallen-in-love, put them into a functional brain scanner, tried to identify what part of their brains were being used, and compared these to other brain states.

Although the researchers expected a much more complex response they found that only a very small part of the human brain is active in this kind of love. In this state of love researchers noted high levels of dopamine, one of those pesky neurotransmitters.

Scientists also found that these activated brain areas differed from those parts activated by other emotional states such as fear or anger. The parts of the brain activated by falling-in-love include the ones that *generate the euphoria caused by taking drugs*. Thus the parts of the brain activated by falling-in-love appear to be the same part of the brain which is activated by using drugs. As with other addictions, higher dopamine levels are noted in those parts of the brain. This experience uses the neural mechanisms used when people are addicted to drugs. Neurologically speaking, falling-in-love may indeed be like an addiction.

Interestingly, researchers discovered that the high dopamine levels do not last forever. They drop as time passes and as the caudate nucleus, which is very active in falling-in-love, returns to normal activity. In short, the addiction stops. Falling-in-love ends. The honeymoon is over.

In its place another part of the brain becomes active. This is the anterior cingulated cortex and the insular cortex. It turns out that the longer the relationship, the lower the activity of the caudate nucleus and the greater the activity of the other two parts of the brain.

The Two Kinds of Love

The fact that different parts of the brain are activated supports the idea that there are indeed two processes at work in this thing called love. As noted, the intense emotional craziness of falling-in-love appears to be more like an addictive process; then it recedes and is replaced by another kind of love, which I call "attachment love." This is the warm, fuzzy love found in longer-term relationships.

The longer the falling-in-love experience lasts, the more there is a reduction in dopamine in the pleasure centers of the brain associated with addiction. Again, this supports the idea that we experience two kinds of love. As emphasized, falling-in-love is an intense experience similar to an addiction. Dopamine and particular parts of the brain are activated. But it doesn't last forever. As time passes the dopamine levels drop to normal levels, and different parts of the brain become active in attachment love.

Thus the evidence suggests that there are indeed two kinds of love when we go through the process of getting into a relationship. One is falling-in-love. The other is attachment love.

Francesco Alberoni, an author, also seems to make a distinction between the two. He describes falling-in-love as flying high above the clouds, and the other love ("attachment love") as though one were standing firmly on the ground. He compares falling-in-love to a flower. Attachment love, which follows, is the fruit.

> *"And there is really no point in asking if the flower is better than the fruit or vice versa. By the same token, there is no point in asking whether the nascent state is better than the institution. One doesn't exist without the other. Life is both."*
> *(Alberoni, 1983).*

Falling-in-love is like a white-hot camp-fire that burns brightly and fiercely. But the campfire does not burn this way forever; it changes into a less intense fire, composed of burning coals. These coals are red-hot yet last a long time. Attachment love is like those coals.

The coals can only be rekindled into a blazing fire for a short period of time. Eventually the fire returns to the coals. Similarly long-term relationships can burn hot yet settle down for the long run. Both are beautiful experiences. But they are not the same.

As Francesco Alberoni suggests, it makes more sense to me to view these two different processes occurring during courtship and marriage (or during an on-going relationship).

Why Different Kinds of Love?

Helen Fisher (2003) believes that there are three different kinds of love.

> *"Romantic love, I believe, is one of three primordial brain networks that evolved to direct mating and reproduction. Lust, the craving for sexual gratification, emerged to motivate our ancestors to seek sexual union with almost any partners. Romantic Love, the elation and obsession of "being in love," enabled them to focus their courtship attentions on a single individual at a time, thereby conserving precious mating time*

and energy. And male-female attachment, the feeling of calm, peace, and security one often has for a long-term mate, evolved to motivate our ancestors to love their partner long enough to rear their young together."

The three exist independently of each other, though there is some overlap. They have their unique emotional and motivational systems, and different chemicals and parts of the brain are activated by each separate kind of love. According to Fisher, these separate loves enable humans to accomplish different things, namely, mating, pair-bonding, and parenting.

In her view, romantic love (falling-in-love) involves concentrating on a single prospective mate. It involves feelings of exhilaration, intense passion, and obsessive thoughts about the partner. She notes that this kind of love is unstable and is not good for raising children, because of its instability.

Long-term attachment love is the final stage of love. This is characterized by a feeling of calm, security, comfort and emotional union between the partners. It can last indefinitely and is the on-going basis for marriage.

Many people make no distinction between the two, yet believe they are a seamless unity. Even though both forms of love can exist in one person simultaneously, the two are very different experiences.

Problems with Falling-in-Love

There are a number of problems:

- ♥ Many lovers cannot accurately assess their partner.
- ♥ Some lovers tend to confuse falling-in-love with attachment love.
- ♥ Some lovers become addicted to the highs of falling-in-love.

- ♥ Lovers believe that falling-in-love never ends; and leave their partners when the intense feeling is gone.
- ♥ Because of cultural expectations, lovers don't accept the reality, importance, and power of attachment love.

Falling-in-Love is Blind

Fred told me that he had put his beloved on a pedestal. She could do no wrong. She did not have warts, only beauty marks. From his point of view, she did not have a wicked temper but was simply assertive. Her angry yelling and name-calling merely reflected some stress which presumably would pass quickly.

Under the influence of falling-in-love, Fred's partner becomes a goddess. He was unable to clearly see and evaluate her strengths and weakness. Since he could not see her weaknesses, he could not accurately predict what it would be like to live with her for any lengthy period of time. The bright shining love covers up the beloved's faults and blemishes. It hides any differences in values, attitudes, and beliefs, and effectively blinds a person from correctly evaluating these things.

Difficulties arise. The entire screening process becomes seriously distorted. Emotions are so aroused that it becomes difficult to accurately assess what the other person is truly like or what is happening to oneself. Many individuals literally don't know what they are getting into.

Since the expectation is that falling-in-love is the only and best prerequisite to marriage, the smitten one may not even realize that other, more rational approaches are available and necessary. Mistakes in judgment are inevitable.

When the love-bug bites hard, our perceptions of the other are distorted. We are unable to see the reality behind the façade; and it's almost impossible not to obsess about the person and ignore all those things, small and large, which might pose problems for us later on.

What can you do to guard yourself?

1. Since part of the experience of falling-in-love is to aggrandize the beloved, it's important not to get carried away by one's feelings. Check things out with your family and friends. Ask them how they see your beloved. Share your ideas and see if they see things the same way.

2. During this period of time, take a pre-marital class. Take one that focuses on attitudes, patterns of behavior, and beliefs. You can use this new insight to discover more about how your beloved and you are different. See if you really know him or her as well as you think.

3. Think about your beloved. Make a list of traits and behaviors which irritate you. Think seriously about them. You may be living with them for the rest of your life. How will you respond to these things five years from now? *Can* you live with them? It's a good question, because your beloved is unlikely to change.

   No problems, at all? That is a cause for concern. No one is perfect or is a perfect fit for you.

What do you do when the highs fade away? Will you still like the person? Do you really have anything in common? Have you developed attachment love for each other? Simply put, falling-in-love is not enough — it's only the beginning!

Confusing Falling-in-Love with Attachment Love

The experience of most people is that romantic love eventually ends. The intensity, the excitement, the desire to be constantly in communication with one's partner, the yearning and pining —it just ends.

Often this phase ends after marriage; but love doesn't really end. People report that they still love their partners, But that it's different: less intense, calmer, saner, and, yes, even deeper.

At this point, some people become very confused. Jim fell in love with Jenny. They eventually married and had a child. He came in to see me because he believed that he no longer loved his wife. He described how the falling-in-love phase had lasted about two and a half years. It lasted long enough for the court-ship, the marriage, and a baby. Then it went away.

Jim was totally confused by what had happened. He no longer yearned to spend every minute with Jenny. In fact, he regained his desire to spend time on hobbies and with his own friends whom he had neglected in the past few years.

He did not particularly want to leave Jenny. Yet he could not help but feel that maybe he should. He no longer was as passion-ate about her as he was before the marriage. In all honesty, it seemed that he no longer loved her the way he used to love her.

He still cared for Jenny, very much. He was attached to her. But he could not help but think that he was missing something. He had lost what he had before with her and wondered whether maybe he should find it again, with someone else.

Even though he had a strong love for his wife, Jim had no idea that attachment love existed. Jim's work with me was for him to realize and accept the love he had in his marriage.

Searching for Highs

Jeff had divorced his wife of twenty one years. Together they had two sons. He left her for another woman. As part of the divorce, Jeff gave most of his assets and income to his family. Clearly, he felt incredible guilt. He loved his wife, but did not feel that he truly was "in love with her." He tried to fall-in-love with her again. They even went to see a marriage counselor. He did feel very close to her and cared for her, but he was never able to again feel what he felt at the beginning. He wondered whether he ever truly loved her. So he gave up and started looking for another love.

He met someone who seemed to completely match his dreams of intimacy and love. She was his match made in heaven. She met all of his criteria for romance and charm and love. He fell in love with her, left his family and moved in with her. But they split up after several months of living together.

Some marriage experts seem to try to rekindle this falling in love for the couple. They try to recapture or reignite the highs of that experience through the work that they do. But it really doesn't work. It's doomed to failure because falling-in-love is time-limited and invariably ends.

Jeff gave it all up because he believed that falling-in-love was the most important thing in life. In a way, Jeff became addicted to falling-in-love — to the intense highs and the sweet emotions. He could not let go of them and settle for the attachment love that was present.

But I Love Her

There is much evidence to suggest that the two types of love are independent of each other, though we can even experience both of them simultaneously. This can be a problem if our attraction is for different people. Men and women can feel attracted to people other than their partner, even while feeling affection and attachment love for their partners. Just because the second kind of love is present, doesn't mean that the first one won't appear. It doesn't have to be acted upon. It's just there.

It's not uncommon for people to feel the romantic love (falling-in-love) for others despite one's attachment love for his or her spouse. Sometimes even the most committed and attachment-loved spouse may feel a romantic love for someone else.

Of course, this is very confusing and threatening for some people. The common belief in our culture is that there is one kind of love, which is directed only to your partner. But your spouse might feel "love" for someone else. All of us are capable of loving more than one person. All it means is that another part of our emotional and physical love system is being activated.

Yet just because it's there doesn't mean that you have to act on it. Falling-in-love is simply a kind of emotion, like anger or sadness. All emotions can pop up anywhere and they all end. You don't have to take it seriously, if you don't want to. All you have to do is concentrate on and choose what is most important in your life. If you have a solid relationship with your partner, it's easy to concentrate on him or her while ignoring any fleeting attraction to another. But it's harder to turn away from these feelings when the home fires are weak or non-existent.

What's Left When the Dust Settles?

Sometimes, when falling-in-love ends, nothing is left. People find out that they have nothing in common. Their values are totally different. They want different things in life. They like to do different things. They have different senses of humor. They don't like each other's friends. Perhaps, initially, they just got caught up in their emotions. But for many there is more there: friendship, affection, caring. Hopefully the coals of the fire are still hot.

In a sense, the rest of this book is about the coals that are left and how to keep them going; how to fan them so that they stay hot, warming the couple during the cold and dark night.

This involves using skills and adopting attitudes and beliefs and strategies which will encourage the coals to keep burning. It also involves periodically adding some kindling and more logs to keep that important fire going. It won't always burn intensely, but it will keep going throughout the night.

The next chapter introduces attachment love. This is the love which starts during falling-in-love and can last forever.

Chapter 4

attachment love

~∗~

Falling-in-love sets many of us up for marriage. But this love generally ends after two years. For better or worse, many couples are married or living together. Even though falling-in-love ends, it's not the end of the world. By this time, attachment love should have developed. The long-term, quiet, deep, calm love sustains relationships for extended periods of time. This chapter explains the attachment love and how it permeates our entire lives.

Nobody Noticed It

Some things in psychology are really no-brainers. Patterns are there for anyone to see, yet they seem to stay under the radar screen undetected and unnoticed.

For example, have you ever wondered why almost all projects take longer to finish than you planned? At least, this is true for me. The faucet takes longer to fix than expected. The new shrubs cost more. The upgrade to the bathroom costs more and takes longer than I figured. How many new homes, new buildings, new bridges and upgrades of all kinds cost more than planned? So it's not just me. Even professionals with all their expertise often miss their estimate.

Some psychologist noticed this and did some work on it. It's now called the Planning Fallacy. It means, simply, that people have a tendency to underestimate the resources it takes to complete projects of all kinds.

So maybe it's not so surprising that it wasn't until 1969 that John Bowlby first wrote about attachment theory.

Love Was Learned

Before then, people did notice that we human beings are social animals. But for the most part, it was believed that this was a learned process. We hung around people and somehow we learned to be social. We learned to be close to our parents and caregivers.

However, Bowlby noticed that many species of mammals seemed to "hang around" their parents in ways quite similar to the ways children are attached to their parents. He documented many examples of baby animals that seemed to automatically stay close to the parent. He concluded that we are not that much different.

Attachment Love is Genetic

We are genetically programmed to attach ourselves to our biological parents or whoever happens to be our caregiver. (From this point on, whenever I use the term "parent" or "caregiver," it refers to any caregiver with whom a child has attached him or herself. It could be a step-parent, a foster parent, the grandparents, or whoever takes care of the child on an ongoing basis.) This explains why we develop close relationships with caretakers. Genetically we are programmed to do so.

We, and the other species that have these attachment genes, are fortunate. As becomes apparent, it made it easier for people to survive.

What Exactly Is This Attachment?

There appears to be a general consensus that there are four general characteristics of attachment. In the next sections, these aspects of attachment are explained.

They are called:

1. Seeking Closeness
2. A Secure Base
3. A Safe Haven
4. Separation Protest

Seeking Closeness

The major aspect of attachment love is "seeking closeness" or "proximity seeking." With relatively few exceptions, people of all ages try to achieve and maintain closeness with their attachment figure. We try to establish and keep in contact with moms, dads, grandparents, children, foster parents, step-parents, mentors, friends, and other people. We are social animals who genetically need to be around people. We want their attention and their help in a variety of ways.

But attachment love is different than our relationship with a store clerk or an acquaintance at work. When we have attachment love for someone, there are specific qualities and behaviors involved. The attention has to be of a certain kind.

A Secure Base

The second aspect of attachment is called the "secure base." Have you ever noticed an infant interacting with its caregiver? An infant will typically explore a room or place and make contact with family members, other infants and kids, toys, even the dogs and plants. But up until a certain age, the infant won't do this unless a parent is physically present. If the parent is absent or can't be seen, the child will tend to get upset. When the parent reappears, the infant will check in and then begin exploring, again.

The younger children stay close to their parents. They explore only in the immediate vicinity. It seems the child has to make sure that he or she can spot the parent. As the child grow older, his or her explorations expand in ever widening circles. Probably because the infant has learned that the parent doesn't disappear when they are not looking, they are now comfortable exploring the room next door. As they grow older, their comfort increases and they explore the backyard, the neighbor's house, school and more. Now my son is exploring California. Next week: Beijing, China?

Seriously, infants need a secure base; a parent, from which they can safely explore the world. We function best in the world when we have close relationships which also serve as a secure base. We need other people who are our foundation or center or support. This allows us to go out into the world with more ease and confidence.

An old phrase goes something like: Behind every successful man there is a good woman. The truth is, during one's lifetime no one individual can be successful without having a secure base in some kind of attachment relationship.

The Safe Haven

When threatened or afraid, an infant will retreat. In fact, the child will run screaming for the parent. It wants to be comforted. The infant wants the caregiver to help him or her feel safety and security. After the child is comforted and calmed down, it will get off your knee and go back to playing and exploring the room and the things in it. This is the "safe haven" of attachment love.

It probably developed as a way of protecting children and infants from dangers. If the kids are genetically programmed to stay close to their parents, they would undoubtedly have a better chance of surviving an attack by a saber-toothed tiger or by the neighboring marauding Cro-Magnons. If the child came running for help, the parents could more easily defend them or snatch them up and carry them away from danger. So it appears to have survival value, making it easier for the tribe and the race to survive.

Of course, it has broader applications for us adults. We turn to our spouses and friends and attachment figures for other kinds of aid and assistance. When I am bothered by something, I will talk to my spouse or my dad or a close friend. In response, this person helps me out both in terms of advice and other kinds of assistance. These are safe havens: people I can go to who help me out when I need it.

Separation Protest

The fourth aspect of attachment is called "separation protest." This means that the infant or young child seeks to be physically close to the parent and fights to prevent separation from one's caregiver.

Parents have often seen these protests. When a parent leaves a child with the babysitter for the first time, the child will cry, cling, call, scream, whimper, hold his or her arms up to us, kick their feet, or do many other things. They are letting us know that their security is threatened and that they want to be physically close to us. This is different than having a temper tantrum at Wal-Mart because they can't have a toy. This is a legitimate and genetically programmed fear of being separated from the parent.

In a sense the infant has two built-in opposing desires. On one hand the infant wants to explore the world. On the other, he or she wants to be close, safe and secure. The two desires balance each other. But when the separation is too great the infant reacts with crying and clinging, protesting the separation from one's parent.

There is a threshold for closeness. When the parent is within a certain geographical range, the child is content and happy. When the child or parent wanders beyond this point, the child will feel afraid and run back to one's caregiver. Because each child is unique, the balance between these two principles varies for each child. Just as some kids are genetically more tolerant of change than others, some need to be closer to caregivers than others.

Stress is also a factor. If a child is tired or sick, he may be crankier and more "clingy" than normal. This is his or her way of expressing one's desire to be closer. Thus when the loved one is too distant, separation protest is activated. It can be triggered by external events. It can also change when the child is either under stress or feeling exceptionally good. But all children share a limit beyond which they will protest and complain and seek your attention. Once that attention or contact is restored, the child feels secure and becomes quiet. The protest system shuts down.

When the Separation Doesn't End

What happens when an infant or child experiences a prolonged separation from the caregiver? Typically, one begins by protesting in some way. But this can't be maintained forever. Eventually, though it may seem to take forever, the child becomes tired of crying. The child withdraws into what looks like a depressed state. The child appears passive, sad, disinterested in the surroundings and seemingly lacks any desire to play or explore. If the child is reunited with one's parent during this phase, he or she appears unusually anxious and clingy.

If not reunited, the child eventually resumes regular play and appears normal. But if parent and child are reunited at this stage, the child is detached and aloof, doesn't want to get close or maybe is afraid to get close to the parent. Eventually, if the reunited parent hangs in there and maintains contact, the child will start getting closer to the parent and, as noted, often may become overly clingy and anxious.

This complex reaction to separation is probably a predictable reaction for both children and adults. First there are protest behaviors. This is followed by clinging to the attachment figure when reunited. If there is no reunion, then despair and depression occur. Finally the person detaches from the person he or she was once close to.

Attachment is Universal

The desire for closeness, a safe haven and a secure base is almost universal. These behaviors can be seen and observed in children, in adolescents, in adults, in their friendships, in their relationships with parents, and with significant others of all kinds. Attachment love is a part of our entire lives, from the cradle to the grave. It influences numerous aspects of our lives.

The absence of the desire for attachment is notable. Some, like those who have forms of autism, lack any such desire. The inability to display social skills and to attach to others is a major symptom of people with autism. But an inability to attach is relatively rare.

How Do We Form Attachments?

The process of forming an attachment with another is probably similar to what we experience as infants. We seek to be close to someone. There could be a desire for friendship, to avoid loneliness, to pursue sexual interest, to seek out information, to fish for praise, to work on a project, or just to enjoy conversation.

This is followed by a successful interaction. Both parties are satisfied by the interchange and have solved a need or a problem, thus establishing a kind of safe haven between the two. With repeated contact, this may or may not develop. Yet over time people will typically feel safe with each other. Then a secure base might develop.

In attachment relationships between peers, the strength of the bond is weaker than in the relationships between child and parent or between intimates. They tend to be less secure, yet they appear to develop in similar ways.

Intimate Adult Attachment

There are differences between us and our children. Children want whatever they see (not so very different than us). They want the security and safety that parents provide. As adults we give this to our children. We end up providing the care, money, support and security our kids need. We do not and should not receive these things from our children. The relationship should be one-sided.

But it's different between adults. Adult attachments are more typically reciprocal. Each partner gives as well as receives in the attachment relationship. This is also true of friends, and for our support networks.

I believe it can be true even between parents and their adult children. This relationship can change in time, with parents and children offering support and emotional security to each other. Certainly, as my parents became older I took on a different role with them; sometimes offering the security of attachment, while asking for and receiving less care. It seems only natural.

So in intimate, adult love-relationships partners offer a secure base and a safe haven to each other. They also generally offer a sexual link, as well. Thus, the attachment between spouses is multidimensional at its core, including mutual giving and care-taking, mutual support and sexual intimacy.

Different Patterns of Attachment

What complicates all of the above is that it doesn't work perfectly.

We learn how to attach and how to complain about separation from our parents, in combination with our own personalities. Parents do not always respond perfectly to what their children need from them. Nor do their children have personalities that necessarily match up well with their parents' strengths. So problems can occur.

There are three different patterns of attachment between parent and child; different ways in which attachments can be handled or lived out.

These patterns are important for a number of reasons. For one, the way our caregiver responds influences the quality of the attachment. It's also largely responsible for setting the threshold for the activation of the separation protest response. Lastly, unless efforts are made to change, these patterns tend to remain the same throughout a person's life. (Believe me, changing is not an impossible task.)

These patterns are:

1. Secure attachment
2. Anxious/ambivalent insecure attachment
3. Avoidant insecure attachment

Secure Attachment

An experiment was created by Mary Ainsworth, an early and noted researcher in this field. Infants were placed in a room. The room contained many interesting toys, one parent and a stranger. The parent was then asked to leave the room, while the stranger tried to interact with the infant. After a period of time, the parent was then brought back into the room. The kids reacted differently to their parents based upon their basic pattern of attachment.

The secure infants were distressed by the separation from their parent. They cried and protested, as we'd expect. Remember, this is called the "separation protest."

When the parent returned, each infant sought comfort from their parent, was easily quieted and then went off exploring the numerous toys in the room. The secure infant fits the normal pattern we described above.

When the researchers visited the secure infants' homes, they found that the parents were generally sensitive and responsive to their children's moods, desires, and signals of distress. The caregivers could interpret these signals accurately. They were warm and accepting of their children. They provided pleasant emotional and physical experiences (smiling, talking pleasantly, hugging, etc.). The caregivers accepted the child's striving for autonomy. They interacted with their children in cooperative and supportive ways rather than in controlling or intrusive ways.

Anxious/Ambivalent Insecure Attachment

The anxious/ambivalent infants reacted differently. They, too, were distressed when their parent left. But when the parent returned, these infants could not be easily comforted or reassured. They continued to cry and fuss and would not easily get back to exploring the room full of toys. Each was preoccupied with his or her parent.

Home visits to families of these kids revealed that their parents seemed to respond inconsistently to their child's signals. Sometimes the parents were unresponsive and sometimes they were overly responsive. These parents were not generally rejecting of their infants; they just did not respond in a way that was useful for the child. Others have suggested that these mothers lacked knowledge, understanding, and skill in how to react to the child. These mothers also tended to be intrusive, being unable to provide clear directions and often entering into a struggle of wills with the child.

Avoidant Insecure Attachment

Avoidant infants seemed not to mind being separated from their caregiver. When the parent returned, the infant did not seek any contact with the parent but kept his or her attention on toys and other things in the room. There was no rushing up to greet their parent.

Home visits revealed that these parents tended to ignore and push away their children. The parents were not close to their child. Some even avoided physical contact with these children.

These caregivers were the opposite of the secure caregivers and tended to be less sensitive to the children's communication. There were more instances of sarcasm, threats, and anger toward the children. In general, they were less responsive, ignoring their children to a greater degree. The caregivers did not express much emotion and tended to control and interfere with their children rather than cooperate in the child's growing ability to explore.

Researchers have attempted to determine how many people have each kind of attachment styles. They learned that the majority, about fifty-five percent, have secure attachment styles; about twenty percent have anxious attachment styles; and twenty-five percent have avoidant attachment styles.

Street Maps of Love

Even as we grow and mature, we tend to keep these styles of relating to lovers, spouses and children.

These differences appear to be maintained and strengthened by our mental representations of them, as though we have an internal street map of how the world works. We build up "internal working models," mental models, of how relationships work and we act accordingly. They are sometimes called "schemas." It's like a street map in the mind, except that instead of street names and traffic lights we have ideas of how we should act toward our spouses, how our president should act, what to expect when going to Wal-Mart.

These schemas are complicated sets of expectations. We form a working model of how relationships work from parents and other people close to us.

Schema 1: How We See Others

Parents can be responsive or unresponsive. They can be emotionally accessible or not. They can be available or not. All of these things work toward creating a stable model of what to expect from others.

Let me give you a personal example. My father, who passed on a few years ago, cared for me, was passionate about the underdog, respected truth and real justice and gave me many things which I needed to get where I am today.

Yet his style of relating to me was complex. I remember his sometimes wanting to play with me. At other times he seemed distant and unapproachable. Many times he was angry. He was embarrassed to say that he loved me and rarely was comfortable with any tender displays or expressions of love. In fact, even though he felt much, he rarely displayed much emotion. He could express anger with ease and tended to yell a lot. I was afraid of him and tended to avoid him. He had few friends and did not trust many people, if any, beyond his wife and kids. He was angry with many people for the things they did to him. This attitude carried over to the world in general.

These attitudes carried on into my relationships with men, especially. I expected them to be angry. I did not trust them. In general, I did not try to get close to them. I was unresponsive to overtures of friendship. I believed that I could not trust men. My mother recently told me that I was an "angry teenager." I suspect that, like my dad, I was also very angry at the world.

As I look back I see that I was just like my dad in many of the attitudes I had about the world. His attachment relationship with me had a big influence on my life. I expected the world to act as he did. Similarly, parents and caretakers unconsciously mold the way their children see their loved ones. Kids develop schemas based on how their parents relate to them and on how they express their attachment love.

Schema 2: How We See Ourselves

The second part of the schema involves how we see ourselves. This is the classic psychological language of self-image. We also gain a working model of ourselves from the attachment relationships we have with our parents.

Many times, in my practice, people have linked their present attitudes about themselves to the way that their parents related to them. Barbara recently asked herself how she became a "good girl" who tried to please everyone. It turned out that her parents tended to ignore her or, occasionally, yell at her. They were not mean. Mostly they seemed to ignore her.

Thus she tried to get her parents' attention by pleasing them, by being a perfect child, by going out of her way to do things for them. If she succeeded, it proved that she was loveable. Of course she never really succeeded. Despite all of her efforts, they ignored her.

However, Barbara kept this pattern of behavior. Since all of her efforts to succeed with her parents failed she also held onto the idea that she wasn't loveable. She is now in her fifties and has finally realized that her self-image derived from her parents' distance.

We respond to our caregivers' style of attachment by forming ideas of ourselves based upon their style. There you have it. Attachment is part and parcel of being a human being. It involves seeking closeness with another person, who offers you a secure base and a safe haven. When your partner seems far away, you respond by protesting in some way. There are three basic styles of attachment, and we bring to the relationship our unique roadmap of love.

But you have yet to see the best. When we have a secure attachment love, there are numerous benefits. These are explored in the next chapter.

love is a many-splendored thing

What about this attachment love? Is this a new kind of love? Why should you go for it? What is in it for you? This chapter explains in more detail the reality of attachment love. It also gives an amazing list of benefits to those couples who enjoy it.

Is It a New Kind of Love?

It's not a new kind of love but it's the king of loves. It's another way of looking at the intimate love between two people and understanding it more fully. This is different than the earlier, more intense falling-in-love. It's a love based on securely attaching to your partner. It's a love based on being a safe haven for your partner. It's as though you and your partner were best friends and more.

It doesn't involve a quid-pro-quo, where I give you something if you give me something. Too much of earlier marital therapy literature emphasized this contract approach to marriage. I give you something but only if you give me something in return. Therapy would then emphasize this kind of bartering.

This could lead to some ridiculous situations (at least, to my way of thinking.) In one example I read about, a husband wanted more (and a particular kind of sex) from his wife. The therapist got the wife to give him this sex in return for new furniture. It might be fun in the short-term, but how much furniture can you afford to buy?

This is not my idea of what a relationship should be like. Couples do negotiate for some things. But it's not the central feature of the relationship. If it is, they can't be all that close.

A Close and Trusted Friend

For our purposes here, attachment love is a secure attachment bond between couples. Like the attachment we had with our parents, it is characterized by a sense of safety, of support, and of physical and emotional responsiveness.

This love is like a close friendship. The one thing that many of my clients miss is a close, supportive friendship with their spouse. When asked, they almost always say that they once had it. They once were able to talk to each other, to share, to listen. Once they felt that the other was close and would accept them. They once felt loved.

The list of benefits to being in a solid attachment love relationship may amaze you.

Independence and Uniqueness

Sometimes men, in particular, are afraid of being too dependent on their partners. My view of love challenges some North

American views of dependency. We like to think of ourselves as rugged individualists. I remember growing up watching those great old-time cowboy movies. The strong silent cowpoke overcame all adversity and then rode off into the sunset, alone.

It seems to me that men, in particular, tend to remain more aloof, more unemotional, more independent, and more likely to not seek support from others. We relax and lose ourselves in physical hobbies and sports, at best, and in alcohol and other drugs, at worst.

I remember being cautious about even being close to my significant others. I was afraid of being engulfed and of being too dependent upon her. I tended to remain vigilant about not getting too intimate or too emotional with my spouse. I kept my distance.

Yet the view of attachment love shown here presents a different picture. Closeness and dependence is natural. It's not only OK; it's essential for greater success.

In order to be truly independent in the world a person needs to be dependent upon one's significant other, at least for a period of time. In a sense, dependence and independence are two sides of the same coin. Each is in tension with each other. One side sometimes predominates, yet can't exist without the other.

Some people argue that there's no such thing as being overly dependent on someone. They believe that couples must find the "right" kind of dependence on each other. For them, the more securely and properly attached you are to your partner, the more separate and unique you can be. It's kind of a paradox. When you are properly attached to your significant other, you become more unique.

Greater Relationship Satisfaction

This is not merely a dream or a fantasy goal. It's real. The research in this area clearly shows that secure attachment love leads to higher levels of intimacy, trust, and satisfaction. People securely attached to their partners report better adjustment to each other and greater happiness.

Inner and Outer Worlds Become Manageable

When people have a connection with a significant other, their inner and outer worlds become manageable. Perhaps the best way to prove this is by illustrating the opposite. Imagine that one of your significant others has abruptly left you. (A significant other could be a close parent, a spouse, a friend, a boyfriend, a girlfriend – anyone who is close to you.) Imagine that this person is gone. He or she died, abandoned you, had an affair, or went to Brazil with no intention of coming back.

How would you feel? Most people would feel devastated. They might be hurt, angry, depressed, or all of these in a whirl-wind of emotions. People have told me that their world turned upside down. Often one feels intense anxiety. This person can't sleep at night. He or she can't seem to concentrate and may feel confusion about what happened, about themselves, about why one is even in the world. He or she goes to work and stares at the computer all day long, accomplishing next to nothing.

When my father died, even though I was expecting it for a few years (he had a heart condition), it was as if I walked into a fog. Things and events I would normally notice slipped past my awareness. I seemed preoccupied with something tugging at my mind; turning me away from the things I needed to do although, I wasn't even sure what it was that was pulling me away. Nothing was clear or easy. My emotions would capture me and run riot for awhile. No matter how small or insignificant, any additional stress that was placed on me easily overwhelmed me.

I remember almost yelling at a cashier one time because he had accidentally charged an item twice. It really was no big deal, because I caught it before I left; yet I could not deal with it calmly. During that time some new paperwork was introduced at work. I remember angrily reacting to it and complaining loudly to the management. Looking back, it actually made my work a little easier; but at that moment, it was just too much to deal with. Others have felt similar things after the discovery of a spouse's betrayal. We experience these things because we have lost our secure base that gives us a sense of security.

When this foundation is disrupted or crumbles, we react in the ways I described above. It becomes more difficult to lead our lives. Our inner, emotional lives become hectic and negatively emotional with turmoil and tumult. Our outer lives become tougher to manage. It's no longer possible, even for awhile, to function at an optimal level: our abilities — to be parents, good spouses, to perform adequately at work — all deteriorate. It can't be helped. Our secure base was disrupted or eliminated, perhaps forever.

The secure base gives us a platform upon which we build our lives.

Secure base and exploring and learning in the world

When you have a secure base, it's easier to explore and engage in the world. One study found that there is a relationship between adult attachment love and one's life and success in the world. People who have a secure attachment love enjoy their work more, are more successful, even take more enjoyable vacations. Healthy and secure love attachments help people to function optimally in the world.

Jeff, a client, told me that he could not have given up the job he hated without knowing that is wife was there, supporting him. She was his secure base and this helped him tackle new things in the world. When our attachments are good, our significant others allow us to engage in the world in creative and satisfying ways.

Secure base and meaning in life, self, and others

When people are secure in their relationships, they tend to have predictable and more positive views of themselves and of others. They tend to see others as dependable and trustworthy. More importantly, they tend to see themselves as loveable and deserving of care and good relationships. These persons are more upbeat about themselves and others. Being, and having been, in a secure relationship, one feels better about oneself. An optimistic self-image is an important benefit.

People with the other attachment styles tend to have more negative self-images. The person with an anxious attachment style is more preoccupied with his or her partner. This person idealizes the relationship and is more dependent on the relationship.

People with avoidant styles tend to avoid intimacy. One is either so afraid of others that he or she pulls back and refuses to interact, or one denies the need to interact. Avoidant and anxious attachment styles tend to be associated with loneliness, anxiety, depression, low self-esteem, self-consciousness, anger, resentment, suspiciousness and fear of negative evaluation by others. Avoidant styles are also related to excessive alcohol consumption. Since such individuals are poorly equipped to handle these problems, anxious and avoidant attachment styles place people at risk for a variety of problems.

Solving problems and argument

Couples in a secure attachment love relationship are able to solve problems more easily. When a couple has long-term and serious difficulties, there is a tendency for great emotion to arise. Anger and pain rule the day. These powerful emotions interfere with the couple's ability to solve even minor, insignificant day-to-day problems. They end up arguing over seemingly stupid things.

Couples with secure attachment styles tend to use strategies such as bargaining, reasoning, and talking. Not least, they trust each other. The couple tends to respond more openly; each avoids trying to coerce or force the other partner to an agreement. One doesn't readily reject the other and is more open to collaborating in seeking a good resolution. There is a high probability of a productive and satisfying solution.

Those with an avoidant style of attachment have a tendency to react to arguments in one of two ways. Sometimes this individual simply refuses to talk and may sulk or leave. Or he or she may ignore one's partner and simply do whatever one wishes.

Secure base and communication

Partners in secure relationships are comfortable about communicating directly and openly with their partners. They are more readily able to tell their partners about themselves, their points of view and their problems. They are able to do this in a way which doesn't shut their partner out.

Secure people can openly admit their distress and fear and turn to their spouse for support. It makes them more resilient in a crisis. It also makes them less likely to be depressed when relationships are not going too well.

In distressed relationships, it's not unusual for a spouse to attack one's mate while complaining. In secure relationships, this is not common. The complaint is handled directly and without difficulty.

In secure relationships, even when a complaint is made the partner is less likely to respond with anger and defensiveness. Couples are able to respond creatively to the partner's concerns, thoughts, and feelings.

A sense of confidence is built up between the couple. There is a conviction that one's partner will listen and respond in a reasonable, productive way. There is a secure knowledge that one's partner will not overreact if he or she shares what is actually on one's mind.

Secure base and processing information effectively

In all relationships there are times when people say and do things which irritate their spouses. Sometimes, for example, I have been known (I confess, it's true) to come home in a cranky mood and start getting down on my family.

A spouse in an insecure relationship might immediately respond in a negative way to the situation above. She will take the anger in a personal way, feeling hurt and possibly reacting angrily or defensively. Perhaps she will think that he is purposefully trying to hurt her. She may think that her spouse is a total idiot for his actions.

A spouse in a more secure relationship will process this information differently. She will think that he is tired and grouchy from a bad day at work. She will avoid any temptation to think that he is doing it on purpose to irritate her or demean her.

People in secure relationships also tend to be better able to consider differing perspectives. Thus even when one's spouse has what at first seems like an idiotic idea, the partner is more likely to seriously consider it.

Actually, couples rarely have the same points of view. This can cause much hardship, difficulty, and fighting. A couple in a secure relationship is better able to see and appreciate each other's point of view.

In general, insecure relationships seem to be associated with more difficulty processing new information, greater difficulty taking in new cognitions and difficulty dealing with emotions.

Businessmen and women sometimes talk about "thinking outside the box." Secure attachment relationships promote this kind of thinking and processing in couples.

Safe Haven and Stress

Infants and adults became calmer when they are in close physical proximity with the significant other, one's attachment figure. (Of course, this is only true if your wife is not mad at you.)

But seriously, when things are going well   or even when things are not going the best   we are genetically programmed to calm down when we are with our attachment love. Our brain literally changes in our partner's presence.

Maybe this is why some people sleep better when their spouse is present. My wife says it's as if she had a security blanket. She finds it easier to calm down and go to sleep. Maybe this is why some people are more relaxed when they sleep with their spouse or why they feel more anxious when the spouse is away. The core of adult love is based upon having a partner who is a secure base and a safe haven for you. It may include a good sexual relationship, but it's more than that. It generally includes mutual sharing between *adult* partners.

When this attachment love is mutual and is truly safe and se-cure, it creates many benefits in the couple's life. These include:

- ♥ More easily managing and controlling one's emotions
- ♥ More easily functioning in and managing one's outer world, including work
- ♥ Dealing more easily with stress
- ♥ More easily exploring the world and trying new things
- ♥ Having a more positive self-image
- ♥ Having a more positive image of others
- ♥ More easily solving problems with a spouse
- ♥ More easily working out arguments
- ♥ Communicating more easily
- ♥ Processing information more effectively and quickly
- ♥ Increased marital satisfaction
- ♥ The decreased probability of divorce

Why wouldn't anybody want these things?

Unfortunately, the ability to form a secure attachment love is not always easy. In the next chapter, we look at threats to attachment, at the different attachment styles which interfere with security and with attachment injuries.

Chapter 6

threats to love

❦

Couples fall-in-love, get married or live together and expect to live happily ever after. The intensity and craziness of falling-in-love ends. Love usually is still there, but the arguments weaken affection.

Does it seem as it your spouse is always attacking you? Does he or she seem to be saying that you are a bad person or that you can't do anything right? Do you defend yourself constantly? Does resentment, anger, and sullenness seem to be growing stronger?

Maybe you can't help complaining. Your partner is just too much for you. Or maybe your spouse just ignores your complaints. The end result is the same. You get upset and angry because your spouse just doesn't "get it." Things go from bad to worse. The arguments intensify and occur more often. As time goes on you become increasingly frustrated. You both become stuck in a cycle of arguments, and often overreact to events. Everything is interpreted in terms of your anger and fear that the relationship is falling apart.

The Real Problem

Remember the basics of long-term attachment love. Couples seek closeness. They form stable relationships that include being a secure base and a safe haven, for each other.

The last part of the theory goes by the odd name of "separation protest." Simply put, one doesn't like it when a partner is distant or if the relationship is somehow in danger. You want to restore the relationship, to make it perfect again. You want to know that everything is OK between you and your spouse.

So one acts or says something to try to make things better and to restore the closeness, but this action triggers the partner to react negatively; this, in turn, triggers the original partner to react, again, negatively. That is the real problem.

Let me emphasize that the fighting and negative emotions boil down to a simple idea — *a partner is upset about distance in the relationship*. A person is bothered by a real or apparent problem with the partner's love. He or she complains in order to try to restore the closeness. But it doesn't work because his or her partner reacts unhelpfully. This, in turn, triggers the first partner to react harmfully or disapprovingly. In fact, the patterns of complaint and reaction occur repeatedly, making it impossible to simply talk to each other.

It all starts with the perception and belief that our love and closeness is being threatened.

Threats to Love

So how can your love be endangered? Actually it's quite easy and happens all of the time. A threat is something that indicates one's partner is no longer emotionally close. It could be an action or the words of a conversation. It could be anything one interprets as introducing distance into the relationship.

The threat involves two things. First something happens or is said. Second, a spouse interprets it as a distance-causing trial.

Let me give you some examples of possible threats.

1. Jim took his wedding ring off early on in his marriage because he did not like to wear jewelry. His wife thought that he was trying to tell her something about the relationship.

2. Because of traffic, Don, my client, was very late coming home from work. It was agreed that he would call his partner if he were ever late. When he continued to be late and failed to call, she became upset and angry with him. He seemed to constantly forget to call and built up a reputation for not calling. Finally she had enough of his disrespect for her.

3. Harry had missed lunch and was very hungry. He thought his wife had a late meeting, and, on the way home from work, he stopped for a bite to eat with a co-worker. When he got home he was surprised to see his wife was already home and that she had prepared a meal. He only picked at his dinner. When she discovered that he'd already eaten, she became upset and angry with him.

4. Jill liked to spend an evening a week with her friends. Her husband, Ken, would become angry with her, accusing her of not wanting to be with him.

5. Cynthia was telling Bill about an event in their marriage which occurred several years earlier. Bill said that he could not understand why she was dragging up old issues and problems. Cynthia became angry because she

believed Bill was blowing off her concerns.

6. Bill became angry. Cynthia told him he was being silly about a worrisome situation at work.

In all of the above, one or the other mate felt an "attachment threat." In those situations, someone thought that his or her partner was more distant, no longer cared for, or doubted or did not respect him/her. An event occurred or words were spoken. The partner perceived that the relationship was strained or made more distant or somehow endangered by it.

This is a threat to attachment love. Your partner seems to say or do something that seems damaging to your closeness.

1. Jim's wife wondered if he no longer wanted to be with her.

2. Don's wife thought he did not respect her enough to call her.

3. Harry's wife thought that he cared more for a friend than he did for her.

4. Ken worried that Jill liked to be with others more than she liked to be with him.

5. Cynthia was upset because Bill could not seem to take her points of view seriously. She believed that he did not respect her.

6. Bill, in turn, could not get any sympathy and support from her. He wondered if she cared for him.

In each of the events above, someone thought that one's partner was more distant, didn't care, didn't want to be with him or her, and didn't respect him or her enough to listen. It seemed that one's relationship wasn't secure, wasn't a safe base, and wasn't a safe haven to share things and get support. These individuals wanted more contact with their partners, their attachment lovers. They were not getting it, so they complained.

Remember, couples are committed to the safety and security of their relationship. When they think it's being threatened, they react.

A Jealous Woman

I recently saw Woody Allen's "Manhattan Murder Mystery." There is scene in which Allen, Diane Keaton, Alan Alda and Olympia Dukakis meet in a restaurant to plan out how to trap Keaton's neighbor into confessing to murdering his wife. Keaton loves her husband, Allen. She also has a crush on Alda.

Dukakis, who plays a writer, gets up to use the restroom. While she is gone, Keaton accuses Allen and Alda of staring at Dukakis, flirting with her, making eyes at her and being in love with her. Both Allen and Alda deny this. They accuse Keaton of being jealous, which she obviously is.

In attachment terms, Keaton is afraid that Allen, her husband, and Alda, her friend, will find Dukakis more attractive than her. She felt that her relationship with them was threatened by this attractive, intelligent new woman who seemed so much better than Keaton. No wonder she complained. No wonder she responded with anger.

Schemas and Maps

But if relationships were all this simple and direct, none of us would have problems. Things become complicated because we don't always act in rational ways. If my wife is three hours late coming home from a night with her friend and has not called me, I will probably be worried not only for her safety but maybe about our relationship. When she eventually comes home, I can respond by:

1. Asking her why she was so late and letting her explain.
2. Attacking her.
3. Ignoring her for a few days.

In a previous chapter, I noted that there are ideas and beliefs connected to our attachment love, called schemas or maps. These patterns of attitudes and beliefs about others and about ourselves help determine my reaction. How I respond to my wife generally depends on my beliefs and attitudes about attachment love.

We generally get these beliefs from parents and experiences in our life. These schemas are not indications of illness or pathology. They are simply learned ways of looking at people who are emotionally close and who are attachment figures. They are not descriptions of a person's personality. They describe how we relate to each other.

Securely Attached

If you are securely attached in your love for your partner, you know you can count on your mate. Relationships and life become easier because the trust is there. You see yourself as loveable and worthy. You can tell your partner what you feel. You can easily talk about any problems which you might have with your partner.

A person with a more secure response tends to be calmer. This individual tends to give his or her partner the benefit of the doubt when there are problems. When he gets home, she will tell him about the missed phone call and calmly ask him about it. Then she will believe him when he tells her that he got involved in his work and simply forgot to call.

Anxious Attachment

If the trust is not there, if there's a "maybe" attached to one's partner, then things are seen differently. These anxiously attached people are not entirely sure that they can count on their partners. They are not sure that they can completely trust *any partner.*

These folks take a different approach to life. As with children, these people tend to either cling to one's partner or aggressively demand the partner's attention. He or she may accuse the partner of imagined infidelities and may demand to know why the partner is five minutes late from work. This person is anxious and nervous about being left alone and wants to be called at all hours of the day. If a spouse should happen to miss an expected check-in phone call, he or she will hear about it on arriving home. This person is more vigilant and very sensitive to any suggestion that his or her partner might be more distant. He or she is more clingy and often more aggressive in demanding explanations and reassurance. When he tries to tell her about his hectic day, she will not believe him. He'll have to work hard to convince her that he merely forgot to call. He will have to work hard to convince her that he doesn't hate or dislike her and that he wants to be close to her.

In short, these individuals are extremely fearful of losing their relationship and may aggressively seek to maintain it. If I had this schema, I would probably angrily demand an explanation from my wife. When she tried to give it, I would probably not believe her.

An Avoidant Style of Attachment

If a person believes that people are not trustworthy, he or she will generally have an avoidant attachment style. This style is characterized by avoiding closeness and by a fear of closeness with one's partners. After all, if people can't be trusted there's no point in getting close. It will only lead to even more pain and suffering.

Life is inherently lonely for these people. They are on their own with few, if any, supports, safe havens or secure bases. Even the desire to be close and form attachments is denied and ignored by people with an avoidant style. This person simply denies his or her need and desire to be close to someone.

If I had this style I would probably ignore my wife when she came home late and probably ignore her for a few weeks. I may feel hurt that she came home late but there is no point in telling her. Besides, I really don't trust her with my feelings anyway.

Two Kinds of Avoidant Styles

Recently, some observers have stated that they believe that the avoidant style can be divided into two patterns. One is the "fearful avoidant" approach. These individuals avoid attachment because they are fearful of others. They may feel terrified of expressing their feelings for any number of reasons. They tend to have a negative, self-deprecating view of themselves.

A spouse with this attachment schema will probably be surprised if her husband called her at all. And if he didn't, after he said he would, it would only confirm her belief that he can't be trusted anyway. So why be upset?

The second kind is a dismissing avoidant style of attachment. People with this style see themselves in very positive terms. However, they deny all need to be close to people. They choose not to be close to others and do not seek it.

An avoidant attachment spouse also will often not respond to one's partner's request for help and assistance and comfort. When faced with a request, this person has a tendency to shut down, become quiet and attempt to withdraw from the situation.

In a previous relationship, I remember trying to talk to my significant other about a problem. After listening to my concern for about two minutes, she turned around, walked up the stairs to her bedroom and shut the door. She was probably overwhelmed, did not know what to say, and withdrew. At the time I had no idea why she simply left. She never did tell me. I bet her attachment style was an avoidant one.

Your Attachment Style

Everybody has a basic attachment style. Sure, your style can change depending on the situation. Also, people grow. Your style can be different after you work on it.

It's helpful to know your basic style. Below is a short questionnaire. It includes only four statements, yet can give you a clearer idea of how you approach your partner.

Read and think about each statement and how it describes your behavior in relationships. Think, in particular, about your behavior in your current (or past) intimate relationship. This is not about what you are like at work or with friends.

On a separate piece of paper, rate the statement on a scale of 1-10. Rate it 1 if it is not at all like you. Rate it 10 if is very much like you. Rate it between these two numbers depending on how strongly you believe the statement describes your behavior.

Here are the statements:

A. It's easy for me to become emotionally close to others. I am comfortable depending on them and having them depend on me. I don't worry about being alone or having others not accept me.

B. I am uncomfortable getting close to others. I want emotionally close relationships, but I find it difficult to trust others completely or to depend on them. I worry that I will be hurt if I allow myself to become too close to others.

C. I want to be completely emotionally intimate with others. I often find that others are reluctant to get as close as I would like. I am uncomfortable being without close relationships. I sometimes worry that others do not value me as much as I value them.

D. I am comfortable without close emotional relationships. It's very important to me to feel independent and self-sufficient. I prefer not to depend on others or have others depend on me.

Your Answers

In these kinds of questionnaires, there are neither correct nor incorrect answers. Everyone is different. That's what makes life interesting. Simply note which of the statements you rated high. The highest is probably your dominant style.

Statement A describes a person who has a secure style of attachment. Statement B depicts a person who has a fearful avoidant style. Statement C portrays the anxious style. Statement D expresses the dismissing, avoidant style.

I suggest you give the statements to your current and/or past partner. Ask them to rate you. This can give you another point of view, which might prove helpful. The more data you have, the better.

By now, you can probably see the problem. Because of your beliefs about people, you can't always stay calm in the face of threats to closeness. Your fears and anger are triggered. When you express these things, you then trigger a response of fear or anger in your partner. This in turn triggers more in you.

So it goes, on and on, escalating into a big argument or a blowup. You get caught up in your unique couple "Dance." When this happens, little communication occurs (except that you may end up hating each other). You both feel hurt and upset and even more distant from each other. Worse, a few days or a week later you have the same argument all over again.

This dance is not always destructive to a relationship. If the couple gets along well, the partners may only fall into it occasionally and then manage to make up. But sometimes significant events trigger the dance. These events may be seen as injuries to love. The next chapter focuses on these injuries.

Chapter 7

injuries to love

In the previous chapter, I explained how threats to love cause people to respond. These threats could be almost anything. They are actions or words which cause your partner to feel more distant from you. These things seem to attack the closeness you desire in your attachment love.

This chapter is about injuries to love. *Attachment injuries* are threats, but they are a lot more serious than attachment threats. Most attachment *threats* are relatively small or minor events which couples can talk about and deal with. But injuries can bring to a halt any attempts at repairing the relationship.

> *An attachment injury is a specific type of betrayal that is experienced in couple relationships. It is characterized as abandonment or a violation of trust. It is not a general trust issue; it concerns a specific incident in which one partner is inaccessible and unresponsive in the face of the other partner's*

gent need for the kind of support and caring that we expect of attachment figures...These events, if unresolved, not only damage the nature of the attachment bond between the partners, they prevent the repair of the bond. (Johnson, Makinen, Millikin, 2001).

This event becomes a recurring theme in the mind of the offended partner. The whole relationship is often described in terms of the injury: he can't be trusted; she always lets me down.

If not discussed and resolved the injury creates not only greater distance between partners but leads one partner to question the entire relationship, to question whether it's truly a safe, secure, healthy relationship. If they are not resolved, these attachment injuries very often lead to divorce.

Let me give you an example.

Why Am I Married?

Marge, who was seven months pregnant, was having a really difficult day. She was watching her two sons, aged four and five. The kids were hellions that day. They were not bad kids, just very active and noisy. No matter how much she scolded or played with them, they would not settle down for her. Worse yet, she was feeling physically ill and overheated.

She called Glen, her husband, at work. She pleaded with him to come home and help her. The first time she called he refused to come home. He also refused the second time. When she called the third time, at about noon, he reluctantly agreed to come home and help her.

Marge felt better, just knowing that she would have some relief in the next thirty or forty minutes. Then an hour went by, and Glen never came home. Ninety minutes, and no Glen. Then two hours went slowly by. She became worried and called him at work. Glen's co-workers told her that he had gone home a little after noon.

Marge was sick and worried, now, about her husband. Where could he be?

The hours passed. He finally came home at 7 p.m. almost seven hours after he left work. Glen told her that he had spent the afternoon with his parents.

Marge felt angry, hurt, and betrayed. She felt that she could not trust Glen. She wasn't sure why she married him or why she should stay with him.

Marge told me:

> *"I was really upset. I felt that he totally ignored me. He did what he wanted to do and blew me off. I could not trust him to do what he said he would do....*
>
> *"I asked him how he could do this. He told me it was no big deal. He said that he wanted to see his parents and that is what he did. I was so angry with him. And I yelled at him. But he didn't care.*
>
> *"I was disgusted, hurt, and angry. I lost a lot of respect for him. I felt a lot of distance between us.... After that incident, I withdrew from him. If I needed something done, I just started to work around him. I began ignoring him."*

In the incident above, Marge sustained an attachment injury to her relationship to Glen. She no longer felt that he cared about her. She experienced the relationship as insecure. It wasn't the kind of stable, safe relationship she wanted to have with him. Because of the event above and others like it, she seriously contemplated divorce from Glen. She did not want to live with a person who did not care for her and who wasn't there for her when she needed it.

Being Abandoned

Generally, there are two major themes which are involved with attachment injuries. One theme is abandonment.

The idea of a relationship is that a bond exists that is secure, affectionate, trusting and reciprocal. Each person receives comfort, closeness, and security. There is interdependence between the two people. Each relies on the other and feels that he or she can count on the other when needed.

In the example above, Marge clearly felt abandoned by Glen. He wasn't there for her when she desperately needed him. The attachment injury was centered on his apparent abandonment of her and she could no longer trust that he would be there for her.

It wasn't that Glen blew off some minor event or was late or some such minor event. When she really needed his help, he did not show up. Usually the injury occurs when a partner *desperately* needs the help and the partner is not there, despite repeated requests and pleas for assistance.

Betrayal

A second major theme is betrayal of trust. In the relationship, we trust our partners. Most people promise to be sexually faithful to their spouses. If one partner has an affair, the spouse is hurt partly because he or she feels betrayed. The trust in the other person is broken.

Remember, the specific incident is not what matters. What is important is that the incident led to your partner's strong belief that he or she was betrayed. In attachment love, trust in your partner is central to being a secure base and a safe haven. A betrayal calls into question any trust you might have for your partner.

Circumstances Leading to Injuries

There does seem to be a pattern to when a partner might experience an attachment injury. In general this occurs during times of stress. Many have told me about crises related to childbirth or raising children. Others have experienced them around a miscarriage, loss of a child, or loss of a loved one. Sometimes the crisis occurs when one partner is under stress because of a job, a transition of some kind (like retirement), or physical illness.

It's sometimes hard to predict what might be a potential attachment injury for a couple. People are different. What seems like a crisis to one person is quite a manageable or even a "ho-hum" experience for another. But invariably it's the sense of broken trust which makes the event a serious injury to one's attachment love.

It Matters How You Respond

Even though much depends on how one experiences the crisis, much also depends on how the spouse responds.

There is guaranteed trouble if the spouse doesn't take it seriously. Too often an offender will dismiss the event. It's my experience that sometimes the partner does not care about what is happening to his or her spouse. Often this individual does not consider the impact a behavior might have. More often he or she just doesn't realize what is happening. This person simply has no idea of how an action might impact his or her partner.

Angela and Phil were not doing well in their marriage. They had been kind of distant for a few years. There was also great financial stress in the family. Phil had left a good-paying job to start a business but the business wasn't doing well because of the economy and difficulty with his business partners. For some reason, Angela needed to find some important papers on Phil's desk, at home. She happened to move his briefcase. A pack of condoms fell out. She was shocked because they never used condoms while making love.

By the time Phil got home that night, she was pretty upset, angry and hurt. She did not handle it well, angrily accusing him of having an affair. She interrogated him about his activities. She eventually calmed down and asked him for an explanation.

Phil, who was a withdrawer/defender, blew it by not taking her seriously when she tried to bring it up and talk about it. He first became defensive. Then he tried to talk her out of her feelings. Then he refused to talk about the condoms at all. He simply clammed up. This did not sit well with Angela. In fact, it did nothing to calm her fears about their marriage; it only made her angrier and more upset. She became convinced that she could no longer trust him and it led her to believe that he truly was an evil man.

The Relationship Changes

The attachment injury leads a partner to question the dependability of one's mate. Sometimes it shatters one's view completely. It has a great and disproportionate affect on the relationship. The injury changes the way you view your partner and redefines the relationship.

Earlier today, I saw a couple for the second time. Jerry, an engineer, tends to think and solve problems but doesn't consider emotions very important. Jennifer is more emotional. They have been married for twenty years and have been fighting and bickering. By now Jerry reacts to almost anything Jennifer says as a criticism. Then he withdraws. Jennifer is equally sensitive whenever Jerry raises his voice or is gruff. She either becomes angry or withdraws. This is their couple dance.

He was complaining that Jennifer was always criticizing him and he did not know why she was always so negative. I asked him to ask her what was really bugging her. She told him a few things that happened recently. I knew there was something more. I pressed her. I asked her to explain the real root of the problem, the real issue, what was really getting to her and fueling her anger.

She amazed me. She told a story of something that happened twenty years earlier. She had miscarried her fetus at twelve weeks. She was hospitalized for a few days. On the day after the miscarriage, she had improved physically, and the doctor said she could go home the next day.

Coincidentally, Jerry had planned a long-awaited fishing trip and was due to leave on the day after the miscarriage. He told Jennifer that he wanted to go on the trip. She said okay and he left her.

Jennifer said that although she felt physically better, emotionally she was still distraught and disturbed. She knows now that she should have told Jerry to stay. Understandably, she was too young and upset to think logically. But she could not help but think that he should have known better. She believed that Jerry really did not care for her. He wasn't there when she needed him. He left the hospital and left her alone because he simply could not be counted on. As a result she has often felt alone.

Ever since, Jennifer has had this belief that she could not count on him. It became a self-fulfilling prophecy. If he did anything by himself, it only proved that she was right: she could not count on him. It led to her losing her sense of closeness and intimacy with Jerry. She often felt vulnerable around him. She even promised herself that she would never again be so vulnerable with him. And I would guess that the injury fueled her irritable nagging that he complained about.

Now don't think that Jerry is totally innocent in all of this. He has done some things which show that he has a few things to learn, as well. For one, he refused to discuss the event with Jennifer. He, basically, ignored her. So she never had an opportunity to deal with or change her view of him.

My point is that the researchers are right. An attachment injury does change the way that people view their partners. It creates insecurity and anxiety. This often leads to the creation of a negative spirit and feeling in the partner affected by the event. The events can cause great, sometimes irreparable, damage to the relationship.

Not Just Big Events

Injuries also can result from a recurring pattern of small events. The small things add up to create a theme of abandonment or mistrust.

People I see in therapy often describe a continuing pattern of relatively minor events which seem to pick away at the fabric of the marriage until it becomes threadbare. For example, a wife might state that her husband works, fixes the house when it's needed, and is there for the kids. But he seems to ignore her opinions and always seems to put her down.

Or a man complains that his wife is just interested in money and the kids. She never wants to spend time with him or listen to him when he needs to talk.

Over a period of time, even small events seem to accumulate and make a marriage more difficult to sustain.

Lastly, some couples have had problems with attachment for some time. Over a period of years and for a number of reasons, the relationship has been poor. Then an incident will occur which brings the relationship to a crisis. The event seems to crystallize a partner's thinking and views of the other. The event opens one's eyes, so to speak. All the past smaller problems are reinterpreted in light of the incident. It leads to injury and feelings of abandonment or distrust.

Healing

Attachment injuries can be healed. Sometimes couples do this on their own and sometimes in therapy. It can be difficult and it can take much time. It requires an openness and honesty which many people find difficult. Many emotions arise, including hurt, anger, guilt, and defensiveness. There may be need for another party, the therapist, to guide the process.

Chapter 8

the war dance

The real problem in troubled relationships is how the partners react and respond to each other. In this section, this
pattern is explored in depth. The two major styles of responding, pursuing and defending, are explained.

Infants and children have a need to attach to someone. They
need to have a caregiver who is a "secure base" for them and
who is a "safe haven," as well. When we got older, *these needs did
not go away*. They were transferred to our partners. They became
our main attachment figure.

They became our secure base, our safe haven to turn to when
things were down, and our sexual partner. The caretaking is
mutual. Ideally, couples take turns helping each other.

Difficulties occur when two things are present. One, something threatens your attachment to your partner. Two, you don't
have a secure style of attachment. This results in "The Dance."

Patterns of Response

There are only two ways that a person can react to his or her mate's distance or separation. One can either complain or one can withdraw. The first one is called the Criticizer/Pursuer response. The second is called the Withdrawer/Defender response.

Criticizer/Pursuer

Anger is the general first response to these kinds of threats. It's a knee-jerk reaction to the threat, to the belief that the partner is gone, or out of ideal contact. People who use this response style complain to their partners. They are hurt and worried about the relationship. So they tell their partners. This usually comes out as anger and protest and complaints.

They try to regain the closeness by complaining, sometimes loudly and for long periods of time (from their spouse's perspective). Sometimes, in one's anger, one makes demands of the partner. To an outside observer and to the partner, this person seems to be critical of his or her partner. He or she also seems to pursue the partner, in the sense that he or she doesn't shrug off the problem. Rather, one goes after their partner; he or she brings things up and demands an accounting.

But it's still an attempt by one person to try to get closeness back in the relationship. The Pursuer tries to reconnect with the partner. It's a strategy of complaining to try to get things back on track.

Withdrawer/Defender

The second response style is the withdrawer/defender response. People who use this style tend to detach themselves when they feel upset or feel distance in the relationship. They leave the room, go to the basement, take a drive in the car, or simply ignore the partner. Instead of complaining, this person disconnects from his or her partner. This detachment can last a short time or it can last for weeks.

The withdrawer/defender may also respond to one's criticizing partner by becoming defensive. He or she may try defending one's actions. Sometimes one become angry in one's defense. If the individual finds his or her partner's words and criticism too difficult to take, he or she may end up withdrawing.

The Dance

Typically one partner will be a pursuer while the other is a withdrawer. In our culture, it seems that more women are pursuers and more men are withdrawers.

A less typical pairing occurs when both partners are pursuers. The fireworks really fly in these relationships. Since neither one backs down, these couples have spectacular fights. Each keeps pursuing and pushing, often escalating the conflict higher and higher.

It appears rare that both partners are withdrawer/defenders. Since neither of the couples actually tries to reach out to the other, these relationships tend to stagnate.

Typically, the patterns of the Dance are relatively stable for a couple. One person pursues and/or criticizes while the other one defends or withdraws. Again, this occurs when the couple feels that the relationship is threatened in some way. It's done when one or both sense a lack of closeness or distance from the other.

This doesn't refer to arguments over whether or not the walls need to be painted green. It only refers to those situations in which a relationship threat may be present. Each person is trying to get the closeness and intimacy that is needed, yet each is unable to do so. The couple is not being immature or selfish. Each may be very skilled in relationships, and able to hold a responsible job. But when one's attachment love is threatened, there is a tendency to use a favorite response style.

The simplest and most common one is as follows. One of the partners, Pursuer (P), feels the other partner's, Withdrawer (W), distance. P thinks that W is far away, doesn't like P or is angry. So P complains to W. P pursues the partner, and often the pursuit is not gentle but angry and critical.

The other partner, W, can respond in several ways. It's common for W to become defensive. Or we can withdraw by clamming up, by leaving the room, or even by trying to placate P in some way. Since offense is usually the best defense, W can also attack back.

Of course, you can predict what happens next. P becomes even angrier and pursues even more aggressively. This generally leads to even more withdrawal or defensiveness from W, which just generates more anger in P. It keeps going round and round until something stops them. Maybe W will get fed up and leave the room or the house. Maybe P will give up, withdraw, and not talk to W for the next few days or weeks. Both end up angry, upset, distant from one's spouse and maybe ready to throw in the towel.

It's a dance, of sorts. A very destructive dance. If the issues are not resolved, people check out. They pursue divorce. At best, they feel distant from each other, often angry and upset for extended periods of time. Neither one of these scenarios were what I had in mind when I got married!

It's amazing that people do these dances, yet have no idea that they are in it. For years, I was caught up in it. I knew there was a problem, but could never figure it out. I could see that sometimes I would trigger something in my spouse. I knew that she could trigger something in me. It was obvious that we played off of each others' weaknesses and "hot buttons." Yet I could neither see it clearly nor stop it.

Different Dance Patterns

This dance can get more complex. Sometimes a partner pursues; but at different times withdraws, depending on the situation. Sometimes one gives up entirely on one's partner. He or she no longer tries to get closer. Then it seems like both have withdrawn, each into a world of one's own.

There is a spike in the divorce rate for people married for fourteen or so years. Couples in these marriages seem to have developed parallel lives. Each has different hobbies, interests, and friends. They only talk about inconsequential things. They have become roommates. I suspect that in such cases, one of the partners got tired of trying; then eventually withdrew and stayed in the marriage for the sake of the kids. When the kids get older, one or the other checks out.

The task couples face is to break this dance. It's to replace destructive patterns with new ones which give both of them the secure base, safe haven, and attachment love that they need and want.

Chapter 9

the pursuer

~~~~~~~~~~~~~~~

I am sure you will recognize the next scene. A couple will start out taking about the toothpaste or some insignificant thing. Then something happens and they get into a serious argument. In the blink of an eye they go from minor disagreement to knock-down, drag-out fight. What happened?

There is generally a lot more going on than meets the eye. They are not really fighting about how to put the cap back on the toothpaste.

If you dig down a bit, the dance involves a number of things:

1. Each person has triggered something in one's partner.
2. Because of this, neither person can talk to the partner about what is really the problem.
3. The real issue is their threatened attachment love for each other.

Couples are fighting about their attachment love for each other. They are either trying to make their attachment stronger or get it back. Most of the time, couples don't know what they are fighting about. They don't know how to get close to each other. They get caught up in their Dance.

In the next section, these three ideas from the previous paragraph are explained from the point of view of the Pursuer.

Phil and Jenny

Phil and Jenny have been married for more than twenty five years. After he retired, the couple moved to a home which they built. It's located about one hundred and forty miles from their friends and family.

At first, Jenny was ecstatic about the move. But over the next several months, she gradually grew unhappy. She tried to tell Phil, but he did not seem to help.

Then her mood seemed to change. She started to pick on Phil. She complained about the house, about the fixtures, about how far away it was, about how things were not going fast enough.

Phil, in the meantime, enjoyed his retirement home and the community. He worked hard on the house. It was a priority for him to finish it. He would often start working on it early in the day and finish in the early evening. By that time he was tired. All he wanted to do was eat, relax and watch some TV.

He felt he could do nothing about his wife's complaining, except to get angry. Most of the time he would "just listen to her, take it and then walk away." Sometimes he would get so upset that he had a major fight with her.

When they sat down with me, Jenny said that she could not stand the idea of living with Phil for the next thirty years of her life. Both were willing to accept that they were part of the problem. But the focus was still on the failings of the other. During the session it became clear that they were in a long-standing pattern, one that was present long before the move put extra pressure and stress on both of them.

They still cared for each other, a great deal. They had many years together, children and memories. But they were not "safe havens" or friends for each other. They had gotten caught up in their dance and could not communicate. The dance has been the problem for most of their marriage.

The Pursuer/Criticizer

Jenny was a pursuer. When she was upset with the relationship, she would pursue Phil. When she felt Phil was distant, she would try to talk to him. When this did not seem to work, she became angry, bitchy and critical – sometimes of Phil and sometimes of things in general. She admitted that sometimes she even would pick a fight with Phil just so he would talk with her. Something was better than nothing.

I asked her what the real difficulty was. As you can probably guess, she said she felt lonely. She had left her family, friends and work. She felt lost. So she turned to him more and more; but he "just wasn't there." He just did not talk or share much with her.

Then she realized that really it was no different than before. Phil always was away at work or doing something. She had felt lonely for years. In the past she had compensated by spending more time with friends and family. Now she could not do that. She only had Phil and he wasn't there for her. He did not want to talk to her. She became angrier. Jenny knew she was doing that and found it hard to stop complaining and criticizing him. She was just too angry.

But Jenny never really told Phil how she felt. She never told Phil that she was lonely, that she did not feel close to him, that she missed being with him. All that came out was the anger.

Their Attachment Love is in Jeopardy.

In a way she was asking more than one thing of Phil. On one level, she was upset about the house and wanted some discussion or answers. But this wasn't the central difficulty. On another level, she was saying that she missed him and wanted to be close. This was the real issue.

Let me repeat — Jenny was really trying to reach out to Phil and get closer. She was asking Phil to be closer. But she was doing this with her anger, and he just did not understand this.

Remember the part in the previous chapter about separation protest? When the child felt too far from the parent, it would run back, crying and making a fuss. Then the parent, hopefully, would pay attention to the child and maybe offer comfort. Knowing that things were ok, the child would calm down and go back to playing. Jenny was doing the adult version of this. She was protesting her perception that Phil was distant from her. She was angry because he seemed so emotionally far away from her. Remember, pursuers do this. When they feel some distance from their partner, they pursue, seeking engagement and communication and closeness.

By pursuing Phil, Jenny was trying to get back into contact with him. In her pain and desperation, she was also angry. But the main point to remember is that she was seeking to be close to him.

Don't Call Me Names

Let me give you another example. Terry and Jim were watching the presidential debates. Terry did not like what one of the candidates said about abortion. So she began telling Jim her views. She was even angry about it. Jim heard her out and became tired of it. So he said to her, "you are just a 'holy roller.' " Terry got extremely angry and began attacking Jim.

In our session, Terry said she believed that Jim didn't respect her. In fact, she often felt this way. At that moment, when he jokingly called her that name, she thought that their attachment love was at risk. He no longer was a safe haven. He no longer was her best friend. He was rejecting her. She felt hurt and angry and tried to reestablish the attachment in the classic Pursuer way: angrily attack him.

After we got this out during the session, Terry did an interesting thing. She asked Jim if he thought that her opinion was important to him. Jim said it was important to him.

I asked her what she was really asking him. Terry was able to state that she wanted his reassurance that she was an intelligent person. Jim was perplexed and did not know what to say. Terry was able to prompt him: just say that I am OK. So he did and she felt relieved.

Even in a seemingly minor exchange between couples, there can be other things going on. What was Terry really asking? She was asking Jim to be a safe haven, her best friend, and to give her some reassurance about his love and respect for her. On one level, she was arguing about the name-calling. But on another, more important level, she was protesting the separation, the fear that he no longer loved her. Her argument was a separation protest.

It's easy to miss. You have to keep on your toes.

Does He Really Love Me?

A woman (or man) might feel that her spouse let her down in some way (in maybe even a small way) and start angrily criticizing him. Dig a little deeper and you may find that she feels distant, hurt, betrayed. *She might even feel that he no longer loves her.*

Jenny feels that the relationship is in trouble. She believes that she is no longer loved, that Phil no longer cares for her, and this devastates her.

The angry blaming is a way of saying she is unhappy. Her pursuit is motivated by her fear. It's not a desire for control or for punishment. It's a desire for reassurance that everything's all right. However, what comes across is in the form of angry protest. She can't seem to help it. All she can do is protest, criticize, and pursue Phil. She gets into moods in which she questions him and even clings to him.

The Anxious Attachment Style

I suspect that Jenny has an anxious style of attachment. This means a number of things. These men and women tend to be preoccupied with relationships. They very much desire closeness, and worry about its absence. They feel insecure. They fear that they might receive an insufficient amount of love or that they might be abandoned. What is worse, they are not sure that they could ever restore that lost love. Their fear and insecurity about love drives them. They are unsure about others, and worse, about themselves. Deep down inside, they suspect that they are unlovable. They doubt that they are worthy of love.

Jenny appears to fit this description, above. She ends up being overly-sensitive to any suggestion that her husband is distant. Because of that fear, she pursues him more. She will tend to become angry and even accuse him, unfairly. This is because of her fears that he will not stay close to her.

Hot Buttons

Sometimes couples argue and don't end up in devastating fights. But sometimes they do. What happened? Something your mate said or did triggered you. A "hot button" in you was pushed, accidentally or otherwise. You automatically reacted, without thinking.

Jenny described it that way. When Phil ignored her, she was reminded of old feelings of fear and rejection and loneliness. It was as if she was transported back to the past. It was a past that she was living with Phil, even now.

When asked, she could easily tell stories of how she felt rejected in the past. She had desperately tried to get her father's attention, but always seemed to fail. It was as if these events were still fresh in her mind. An incident with Phil could place her back in the same fearful mood. It was as if she were reliving those moments of intense emotion and pain. Her hot button was that powerful.

This is just half of the Dance. When Jenny reacted, she pushed Phil's buttons. Phil reacted and in turn triggered more from Jenny. This was the cycle. It just keeps going until one or both stalk off in sullen anger.

The hot buttons can be triggered by just about anything. It could be a behavior, words, a tone in your partner's voice, a facial expression (rolling eyes) or even a bodily gesture. When pushed, old feelings are remembered. Old reactions are automatically set off. And the Dance begins anew.

Not Much Trust

If you have an anxious style of attachment, you don't trust very much. There is an uncertainty about your partner. You are never sure that your mate will be there for you. You wonder, a lot, whether he or she truly loves you.

Fear is at the center. Jenny is constantly fearful of losing Phil, which precipitates her pre-occupation with Phil and how he is reacting to her. She overreacts to anything which suggests he is distant from her. She also experiences an overwhelming compulsion for reassurance from her partner. She seems to constantly seek proof that he still loves her and wants to be with her.

Jenny described how she wanted to believe that Phil loved her, yet a part of her could not accept it. Underneath it all, she, and people like her, do not trust that others can or will love them; they fear that they are unlovable.

Jenny said, "I know I get angry with Phil. Yet I don't understand why he stays. Sometime, I wouldn't blame him at all if he left, though it would devastate me."

She believes that she is not loveable. These beliefs about herself stem from her upbringing and experiences. They are not conscious choices for her. It's not Jenny's fault that she believes these things about herself. Nor is it her fault that she has these behaviors. But if she wants her relationship to improve, then she must break her part of the dance.

Layers Upon Layers

Notice that there are layers to this problem.

1. Jenny believes her partner is distant or that the relationship is threatened in some way.
2. She complains and criticizes.
3. Underneath it, Jenny really feels hurt, lonely, and afraid.
4. She feels lonely because Phil seems to ignore her.
5. She feels hurt because Phil seems to be saying that he doesn't like her.

6. When Phil doesn't listen to her, she is reminded of past incidents when she felt ignored.

7. Jenny fears that Phil may no longer love her, that their attachment love is gone.

8. A part of her believes she is unlovable.

9. Underneath it all, she doesn't trust that Phil or any partner might truly love her.

As you can see the argument is really about whether Phil still loves Jenny. It's not about the new house or the cap on the toothpaste. Because Phil reacts the way he does, deep feelings of fear are triggered in Jenny. She has a difficult time explaining these feelings and fears and beliefs to Phil. Instead, she plays her part in the Dance.

It all comes down to belief and trust:

♥ Do you truly believe that someone can wholeheartedly love you?

♥ Do you truly trust that your partner can love you despite your faults?

For someone with this style, sadly, the answer is '"no" to both questions.

In the next section, Phil's thoughts and feelings are portrayed.

Chapter 10

the withdrawer/defender

❧

I t takes two to tango. For every action, there is an equal reaction. The Pursuer is generally matched up with a Defender. In this section, the other half of the most common dance is explained: the Dance of the Withdrawer/Defender.

The Withdrawer/Defender

The withdrawer has a different style. When he or she feels that the relationship is threatened, retreat is the preferred response. Let's go back to Jenny and Phil.

When Jenny criticized, Phil responded in a number of ways. Sometimes he would try to solve problems. This was his preferred method of dealing with Jenny. For example, if she was sad he tried to help her find ways of getting happy. If she did not like that she was away from her family, he would rationally come up with a solution. In fact, he was really good at problem-solving.

Yet it did not seem to work, very well. He could not understand why she never seemed satisfied with his attempts to solve her problems. He was confused and somewhat irritated by it. For despite all his work, she still wasn't happy.

Sometimes, Phil defended himself. When Jenny accused him of something, he would explain why he did what he did. He would reason it out, giving her all his thoughts and decisions which led to a particular behavior. He often repeated himself, because Jenny just did not seem to understand his rationale.

As Jenny seemed to criticize him more and more, Phil became increasingly frustrated and angry. When Jenny continued pressing him, he would blow up at her. Then they would get into a major fight.

Often Phil responded to Jenny by withdrawing. He did this in a number of ways. He went to work, did not come home at reasonable times, played golf, or simply ignored her. When he could not avoid her, he would impatiently listen to her complaints, until he got angry. Then he would become defensive and fight with her. Eventually he would throw his hands up in the air and walk away.

Get Off My Back

In one session with me, Phil got angry at Jenny. He was fed up with the situation. He said that she constantly pestered him. He painted a picture of a woman who continuously wanted his attention and would never leave him alone. (Remember, Jenny had an anxious attachment style.)

He complained that all she did was complain about her life and about him. He did not believe that she would ever be happy, in their new home. He also didn't think it would help to move back to their family and friends. She probably would not even be happy then.

He stated over and over again that he did not know what she wanted. He was sick and tired of being attacked for doing nothing. Phil did admit that most of the time he tried to avoid his wife. He simply did not know what to do to get her off his back.

Beneath the Surface

But much more was going on beneath the surface. Phil knew that he was uncomfortable with emotions. He often did not know what to say to Jenny. He also admitted that when Jenny was angry with him, he felt crushed. He could not handle any of her criticism. Often, his emotions would overwhelm him.

I can't emphasize this enough. Her anger was intolerable for him. He simply could not take it. He had to withdraw to protect himself.

Phil, the withdrawer, was hypersensitive to any criticism from his wife. He feared being criticized and rejected by his wife. So when Jenny became angry, he was at a loss. He had a difficult time responding to his wife's criticisms and anger. He would defend himself, telling her how he did not fail her. But when she did not calm down, he'd get so overwhelmed that he could not even speak to her.

The Avoidant Attachment Style A

There are two types of avoidant partners. I see a lot of men, like Phil, who get defensive and withdraw when their wives complain or criticize them. These emotions are scary and often overwhelming. So it's easier to try to solve problems in an intellectual way. Phil is in this category.

Dig a little deeper and you will find that the desire of avoidant partners to be close to their wives is very strong. They simply can't stand the idea that their wives are criticizing them.

Firstly, the emotions are too intense and difficult to handle. Secondly, they feel that their partners are rejecting them. The third big part is feeling inadequate as a mate. The wife's anger is interpreted as critical rejection. The partner feels as if he's blown it. So the fear of losing his partners is triggered.

Withdrawal is way of regulating the fear. It's a way of avoiding the negative comments which hurt so deeply.

Similarly, these men have a hard time responding to their partner's requests for sharing and comfort. Often, they can analyze and solve problems with ease but simply cannot quietly listen to their wives' feelings. They have a difficult time offering verbal comfort. They simply cannot fathom the reason for doing so.

I do not want to give the impression these men and women are withdrawing in all aspects of their lives. Sometimes they are and sometimes they are not. They can be charming, outgoing people who have jobs involving much interaction with other people. They can even be the life of the party.

But when this person feels that the attachment love of his spouse is threatened, when he feels that his spouse is attacking him, he backs off. He tends to defend and/or withdraw. The style and behavior is triggered only by one important thing: his perception that his spouse is criticizing him. And believe me, an irate spouse can be very critical.

The Avoidant Attachment Style B

The second avoidant style is very similar to the first. These men and women are uncomfortable with closeness. But they appear self-sufficient and may even feel worthy of love.

They do not see others as willing or able to give them what they need. Others are untrustworthy. But they differ in one important way. They accept that they will never be close to anyone. This person does not expect to be an intimate, best friend to anyone. It simply doesn't exist. So why wish for something that can never happen?

These men and women often hold a cynical and negative view of others. They deny that they need to be close to anyone. In fact, they deny having many emotions. To their partners, they appear to be unemotional, aloof, and cold.

But it's all a false front. Experimenters have hooked up these men and women to instruments which measure physiological change. After a fight with their mate, these avoidant withdrawers have just as much physiological arousal as anyone else. But if you would look at them, they appear cool and calm. Underneath, they are upset even while denying it.

Actually this person's need for closeness and attachment love is just as real as that of the next person. Only he denies that it exists.

Hot Buttons

So what triggers men and women who have the avoidant style of attachment? In many cases, it's anger and the belief that he or she has failed his or her mate. This is what happened to Phil.

Phil was describing how difficult it was for him to deal with Jenny's complaints and criticisms. He recognized how he defended or withdrew, yet had a hard time identifying what it was that really got to him.

I asked him what he felt at that moment of withdrawal. Phil said that he did not know. So I started naming emotions: anger, hurt, sadness, fear, etc. When I got to shame and humiliation, he reacted. Slowly, with difficulty, he told us what he felt. He was humiliated and ashamed that he wasn't a better husband to Jenny.

This was a revelation to Jenny. Many withdrawers are really reacting to the implied statement that they have failed. Phil felt humiliation and shame because, as he interpreted it, Jenny was telling him that he was a failure. These complaints triggered old and painful feelings.

When asked about it, Phil acknowledged that he was reminded of his past. He'd had many early childhood experiences which placed an emphasis on competence. He had to be a good businessman, a good gardener, a good father, and a good husband. In fact much of his thinking, self-image, and pride centered on his competence. Phil had a burning need to be good at almost everything he did.

Doubts

But he wasn't totally convinced. He still quietly wondered and doubted that he was all that perfect. In fact, in those moments when he was brutally honest with himself, he knew that he was far from perfect.

When Jenny complained, she inadvertently touched this sore spot in Phil. No wonder he reacted. First, he was overly sensitive to any suggestion that he wasn't competent. Second, it hurt that his wife thought he was less than perfect. Third, his own doubts about himself were activated. No wonder he reacted with anger, objections, defensiveness and withdrawal.

Trust?

Toward the end of one session, Jenny was trying to understand this man who she had lived with for almost thirty years. She observed that Phil had few friends. She also noted that he rarely shared anything with her.

I asked Phil if this was true. I was amazed that he completely agreed with her. I then asked him why this was the case. He stated simply that *he did not trust anyone.*

I pressed him, asking about this. He said that if he shared anything important, anything close, he would get hurt. He was pleasant with his friends, but did not really let them know who he was. He had a wife, but never felt that she was a safe haven for him. He reacted with anger when she criticized him and spent as little time as possible with her. He ignored all of her attempts to get close to him.

Phil was communicating his lack of trust when he distanced himself from Jenny. He did not feel safe with her. When she criticized him, which hurt him considerably, this only proved to him that she could not be trusted.

To be fair to Jenny, Phil did not trust anyone. He was afraid of opening up because he might get crushed. He tried to maintain his sanity by keeping his distance. When pushed, he would fight. But most often he tried to stay safe by withdrawing.

Layers Upon Layers

Notice that there are layers to this problem.

1. Phil hears Jenny complain and either defends himself, withdraws or tries to solve her problem. Sometimes he becomes angry.

2. Underneath it, he really feels hurt, ashamed, desperate, and afraid.

3. He feels hurt because Jenny seems to be saying that she doesn't like him.

4. He feels ashamed because Jenny is telling him that he is inadequate and incompetent.

5. He feels lonely because Jenny is rejecting him.

6. He fears that Jenny may no longer love him, that their attachment love is gone.

7. He may become desperate that she will leave him.

8. He withdraws because he can no longer handle the intense emotions.

9. Underneath it all, he doesn't trust that Jenny or any partner might truly love him.

10. There is a part of him that believes he is unlovable.

Underneath it all, Phil, who is a withdrawer, is remarkably like Jenny. They do not trust that others will love them. Nor do they trust that they are loveable. This is reflected in the last two points above.

Essentially, it's a matter of belief and trust.

- ♥ Do you truly believe that someone can wholeheartedly love you?
- ♥ Do you truly trust that your partner can love you despite your faults?

So each partner lends his or her own unique spin on the dance. Each complements the other in a very negative and destructive way. In the Dance, each mate triggers the other. Arguments, fights and distancing are the results. It ends with a loss of close-ness, which often leads to a separation or divorce.

Chapter 11

closeness and intimacy

‹‹‹‹≈•≈›››

Relationships fall apart primarily because couples are no longer close to each other. They become involved in their Dance, trigger each other's hot buttons, get angry, and build up walls. Trust weakens. Partners grow apart. Eventually, their love for each other is destroyed.

The trick is to stay good friends, no matter what. In attachment love terms, it is to be a safe haven for each other. Some marriage therapists try to accomplish this by giving lessons on how to argue, how to resolve conflict, or how to communicate more effectively. Many of these ideas are useful.

It makes much more sense to concentrate on what works. The ideas in this book are based on Emotionally Focused Therapy for Couples. This therapy was developed by Dr. Susan Johnson, in Canada. Studies show that this therapy is twice as successful as other marriage therapies. Its goal is to re-create the close friendship which couples have lost. It emphasizes the things which are important in re-creating closeness. The biggest one is quite simple: sharing. People grow close to each other by sharing.

Sharing

There are all kinds of sharing. It's said that men bond by doing things together. People often feel closer to each other after they share an emotional experience. If the emotions are intense, the bond can be immensely powerful. I don't know my daughter's father-in-law very well. I felt closer to him when we both celebrated our first grandson.

My client, who was a combat sergeant in Viet Nam, stays in regular contact with the men in his unit. The intense experiences of combat forged this closeness.

Couples can achieve closeness by:

- ♥ Parenting together
- ♥ Developing shared interests and activities
- ♥ Recreating together
- ♥ Engaging in sex
- ♥ Sharing actions based on shared values

Shared experiences can lead to closeness. But the most powerful path to closeness is through emotional intimacy.

Emotional Intimacy

Do you want to be close to your partner? Then start sharing feeling with each other. This develops and maintains close, happy, intimate relationships like nothing else.

In studies, "feeling good" about your spouse is the only thing which predicted marital happiness, satisfaction, and stability. Emotional disengagement signals a marriage ready to dissolve.

Lack of engagement is even associated with the lack of success of traditional marital therapy. If two people don't have some feeling and commitment for each other, the partnership is in trouble. When you and your spouse are no longer friends, you are in trouble.

Sometimes people think that only some emotions should be shared: the right kind. They believe that sharing negative emotions lead to problems. But what leads to problems is the Dance. Partners trigger each others' hot button. This brings anger and resentment on both sides, leading to emotional disengagement. This breaks up relationships.

Certainly it makes sense that positive emotions need to be present for a relationship to survive. But a solid relationship must also include handling the negative emotions, as well.

What Is Emotional Intimacy?

A good way to illustrate the idea is by showing you what it's not. Here are some examples.

1. Jeff came home from work. His wife, Monica, proceeded to tell him about her day with the kids. He listened somewhat impatiently. Jeff really wanted to eat dinner and then work on his hobby. He got the idea that her day was difficult. So he helped more with the kids before he turned to his pastime.

2. At breakfast, Monica and Jeff talked about the kids' schedules. They negotiated who was to take them when and where.

3. Jeff and Monica talked about their finances. They planned what furniture to buy.

4. Monica told Jeff about a conversation she had with her sister.

5. Monica and Jeff had the following conversation:

   M: For the past few weeks it has been hard for me. When you are in a bad mood, after a bad day in the office, I just look and know to leave you alone. And then I feel really distant. And I am kind of afraid to bring it up.

   J: Well, why didn't you tell me then?

   M: Because I know you will be in a bad mood and yell at me. So I try to leave you alone. But it is hard.

   J: I don't know what you are talking about. What do you mean? If I am that way, then tell me (emphatically).

All of these conversations are important. But *none* are examples of emotional sharing.

In the first example, Jeff helps out. But no communication took place.

In examples 2, 3, and 4, the partners either shared information or negotiated. I tell you what my day was like. You tell me about your mother or the kids. We talk about schedules, vacations, what to eat, what to spend and many other things which make up our lives.

Occasionally, the Dance is triggered. Example 5 is an example of Jeff being defensive after his wife complains about him. The conversation ended up with a fight and hurt feelings.

None of the above involved emotional sharing. Then what is emotional sharing? It's a communication with my partner which includes three things:

1. Sharing emotions, with your partner.
2. Your partner accepting your emotions and responding on an emotional level.

If you are trying to improve your relationship, a third point must be present.

3.   You must share emotions which focus on your relationship.

Let me give you a segment from a real conversation between two of my clients. This example illustrates emotional intimacy:

L: *I am afraid that if I got really upset and did not want to work something out when you did, that you would leave me. I am really afraid that you would get angry and would leave me. I guess in a way I don't trust you.*

   I am afraid that if I don't live up to your expectations, if I argue with you, then I am not worth having around. Maybe you will just be gone the next day.

   Will you hang in there if I am a cranky and irritable? Will you love me and still you stay with me even if I get completely angry with you in a fight?

A: *Yes, I would and do. I feel terrible that you are so afraid. That whole thing, your anger, at worse, is a temporary condition. I know you deep down; I know that you are a wonderful person. Yes, I might be angry that night, but the next day I will still be there. I want you in my life.*

A. responds on an emotional level. He doesn't try to talk his partner out of her feelings. He simply expresses his feelings: he feels terrible about her fear. He then answers her question. He intends to hang in there. His response of acceptance powerfully transforms the relationship. It's almost magical, when it happens. When one partner risks and the other accepts, trust is formed.

Why Aren't You Doing This Already?

Couples do not share in this way. The most common reason is that they don't realize it's important. Even when shown how to do it, often they don't share because they are afraid. Afraid of what? Usually, it's a fear of being rejected by your partner. The trust is missing.

Recall the chapters on attachment styles. Many times these suspicions come from past experiences. We go into the partnership with doubts about our partners. We go into it partially believing that it's unsafe to trust our partner.

When our mate acts in some particular way, we interpret the action in light of our doubts. The distrust is reinforced. It grows. For a relationship to succeed, this mistrust has to be countered and stopped. For a relationship to succeed, confidence in the companion must be fostered and grown.

The way to do this is by sharing emotionally with a focus on the relationship. When this happens, safety is created. Often one is afraid to share emotionally. It is taking a risk that your partner will reject you. But when the risk is taken and the partner responds in accepting ways, safety and a little bit more trust is created.

Things can snowball from there. Even a little sense of safety and trust encourages more risking and sharing. Couples can get on a roll, in time, with enough of these kinds of experiences. Now you can share other emotions about other things. This is fine. But this book is about improving relationships. So you need to make the relationship the focus.

I repeat, because it's so important. To improve your relationship with your significant other, you must establish a close friendship. To do this, you must focus on sharing your emotions connected to the relationship.

You've Convinced Us.
Now What Do We Do to Get There?

The answer is simple, yet sometimes difficult to put into play. Two general things must be done. First, you must eliminate some common beliefs and attitudes which get in the way of sharing. Second, you need some skills. Most people will think of communication skills. In fact, there are many books that teach how to fight, how to communicate, etc. But I am not talking about these things. The skills in this book involve emotions and being emotionally close. Most books don't deal with these issues. That's what makes this book different.

Chapter 11 shows how common attitudes and beliefs get in the way of closeness. Chapters 12 and 13 give concrete ways to work on closeness.

Chapter 12

getting closer

ow do we make the relationship last? How do we become best friends?

First, change your attitudes. Then work on some of your emotional closeness skills. This chapter offers several ideas which can help you.

A word of warning, though. Relationships take effort. If things are not going well, concerted effort is needed to change attitudes and behaviors. There is no pill or magic wand to make it all better. But if the commitment is present, it can be done. I have seen it happen many times.

Who Is the Problem in This Relationship?

You are — at least for half of it!

Many readers will disagree. Everyone who comes to marriage therapy firmly believes that his or her partner is to blame for the difficulties in the relationship.

Each is convinced that his or her partner doesn't listen, communicate, love or think of him or her enough. So the aggrieved mate drags the partner into counseling, expecting a fix. The troubles then will go away. Case solved.

To be fair, some do admit that they may have "some" blame in the situation. But I suspect that deep down this person still thinks that most of it can be laid at the feet of the partner. I know this because that is exactly what I thought when I got divorced.

The difficulty lies with how the two relate to each other. It's their relationship that is troubled. Hot buttons are being pushed. Both are being triggered into senseless arguments. Both are doing the Dance.

Unable to talk, couples end up resenting and putting emotional distance between each other. Clearly, each partner brings something to the breakdown. Each is at fault. If you want your relationship to last, accept responsibility for your part. Be humble.

Killer Contempt

You feel miserable and don't know how to fix the problem. Both of you feel even more distant from each other. You spend less time with each other. You begin to wonder whatever possessed you to get married.

Researchers have found that couples create a state of negative emotion between each other. It's so strong that it seems to capture and color their perceptions and reactions to each other. The anger and negativity can be so great that they miss things. They may not even notice that their partner has apologized or is trying to discuss rather than attack, blame, or defend.

Not only is there great anger aimed at your partner, you begin to see each other in only negative terms. He is irresponsible. She is selfish. He only cares about himself. She was never there for me. Worse, you begin to think that your partner has no positive qualities. A spouse will forget that there were times that he did things for her or was available for her. He will mainly remember the bad times and truly believe that there is no good thing that the spouse can do.

He is not just occasionally selfish; he is "always selfish." She is "never there" when needed. You become contemptuous of your partner. The arguing couple tends to interpret every action of one's partner in terms of this negative, global judgment of one's all-encompassing uselessness.

When you are unhappy, it's easy to blame your partner. Unfortunately, it doesn't stop there. Too often, people see each other in increasingly negative ways. Disrespect grows. Eventually partners only feel contempt for each other.

An example. Barb married Cal. Both were barely twenty. Soon, they had a baby. Cal was greatly worried about the finances, so he focused his time and energy on work. Barb complained about his not being home enough. Neither could discuss the situation because both were caught up in their Dance.

After a few years, Cal began to get the message. But by this time, Barb's anger was great. She constantly complained to him or berated him. She even began calling him names and telling him that "nobody would ever love him." She was contemptuous of Cal. He could do nothing right in her eyes. Her anger led to blaming him. Blame led to disrespect and contempt.

Contempt is extremely damaging to a relationship. Not surprisingly, studies show a high correlation between contempt and divorce. If you want your relationship to last, stay away from contempt and blame.

Trying To Get By the Best We Can

Couples need to "cut each other some slack." Each partner should back off a bit. Try to see your mate differently, to see him or her as someone with weaknesses and hot buttons. God forbid, you might even consider forgiving your partner!

Your partner is probably just trying to get by the best way possible. When those damaging fights occur, your partner is really trying to say he or she wants to be loved and wants to be close. But it comes out the wrong way. Your partner doesn't know how to say it. That's right; he or she doesn't know how to say it. But more on this later.

Try seeing your partner in a new light, in a different way. Anger, blame and contempt lead to a dead end.

Dependent on Whom?

Some people shy away from the idea of being dependent upon another person. I can appreciate their misgivings and questions. After all, we've been raised in a culture that celebrates independence. In the movies, which glorify our past, our Old West heroes invariably defeated the bad guys and rode off, alone, into the sunset. They often had a love interest, but rarely settled down.

Today these attitudes and beliefs about self-sufficiency live on in sports and other areas of our culture. Often it's difficult to bond as a team because of the players' concentration on individual statistics and performance.

The Detroit Pistons' philosophy is much different. They attributed their success to a number of things, including a team emphasis. Players depended on each other to help. A recent article in the Detroit Free Press reported that this team even socializes together in order to build the bonds between players. The team literally fosters a family feeling.

Actually we've been dependent on a large number of people and organizations throughout most of our lives. As infants we totally relied upon our caregivers. Infants don't survive without considerable help. We also needed schools and teachers to lead us in learning. True, you put in effort. But you could not have gotten here by yourself. You stand on the shoulders of the people who came before you.

This is equally true for all kinds of disciplines. The 2006 Corvette did not spring into existence out of the minds of current engineers. They are dependent upon the ideas and work of people before us. Even to build this magnificent machine requires the work of thousands of people, who depend on each other to get their part completed.

Our culture prizes independence, yet we also rely we rely on each other.

So what is the hang up about being attached to and relying on your spouse? About the idea of establishing a secure base with someone who helps us achieve what we need in the world? What's wrong with the idea of having a safe haven whom we can turn to?

Dog Eat Dog World

Work attitudes can hinder relationships. Harry, in the previous chapter, was a representative for a major drug manufacturer. He wasn't close to his wife and rarely shared much with her.

Harry told me that it would be suicide for him to open up to people at work. They would chew him up and spit him out. It was a dog-eat-dog world. To show any kind of vulnerability was to invite disaster. His competitors, including other sales reps, would see any show of feeling as weakness. It was a vulnerability which has been used to undermine him both personally and professionally. Thus sharing emotions was impossible for Harry since it meant he would open himself up to pain and injury. This was unthinkable. So he clammed up and stayed professionally distant, even from his wife.

Harry's mistake was to think it was acceptable to treat his wife the same way. He was raised in a nuclear family that encouraged him to hide himself. He worked in a corporate culture which forced him to hide his feelings. No wonder he did not expect his wife to be a safe haven.

He never opened up to his wife. Never! They lived for thirty three years together and never talked about much besides the kids and the weather. No wonder he was always miserable, felt empty, and never had a clue until his wife wanted to leave him. If you believe that it's unimportant to rely on your partner, you're setting yourself up for failure.

Are Men from Mars and Women from Venus?

No. But it does point to another thing which stops some people from fostering closeness with a spouse. It's their style of relating to the world.

Our culture places a premium on the intellectual, thinking, and analytical aspect of ourselves. The best students are those who can remember a vast amount of information, analyze the data, and solve problems. Though these capabilities are important and prized in many situations, they are not always useful in intimate relationships.

John Gray has stated that men like to solve problems. His wife has a problem. Being a good husband, he tries to solve it. Solutions are discussed and offered.

This only causes grief for many wives. They are looking for something different. These women only want their partners to listen and respond emotionally.

Thus men are from Mars (which emphasizes problem solving) and women are from Venus (which emphasizes emotions). Both men and women can be problem-solvers; except that in our culture it seems that more men use this style.

Men, who are great at problem-solving, often miss all the rest. When a mate asks for support, or just wants to talk, these men don't know what to do. When a partner turns to him and asks him to be a safe haven, he can't deliver. He doesn't know how to be a close friend. In fact, he often has no idea of what his spouse is asking of him.

Sheila, an engineer for an auto company, handled technical details quite well. Yet she and her husband were fighting. She did not understand why he was so upset all of the time. She worked hard, made a great deal of money, completed her share of the housework, and wanted sex with him. When he had a problem, she always listened and told him how to deal with it. What more did he want? She could not understand why he was so dissatisfied and always complaining that she was so distant. Her husband wanted an emotional response, but she had no idea what he was talking about.

Listen Emotionally

Sheila did not realize that often she did not have to solve any problems. All she had to do was listen. Sometimes partners have a hard time believing this, but it's true. It's vitally important to listen and relate emotionally. If you're a problem-solver, great. But also take the time to listen and respond on an emotional level to your partner. Often that's all you have to do.

She Is Always Angry

It seems she is always complaining, always angry. You don't understand why. You're tempted to think that there's no pleasing her. You're inclined to "blow her off," again. Then you remember reading something in some book. What was it? Something about "separation protest?"

When Mom and Dad first leave their kid with a babysitter, the child often cries. Baby Judy wants to be close to her parents. So she tries to tell them in the best way she knows how. She cries, whines and complains. This is separation protest. Baby Judy is trying to get close, again, to Mom and Dad.

When you see a threat to the relationship, you tend to automatically react, get angry and complain. Just like our kids. Everybody seems to do this. It's almost a natural law.

Meanwhile, as a recipient of these protests, you often feel hurt and angry and interpret it as a personal attack. You may think you are unloved. You may even believe that your partner has a serious personality flaw. But these interpretations are usually dead wrong. What is really happening? Your partner is trying to get closer. It may not be the best way to do this. It may be confusing for you. But that doesn't change what is happening.

Your partner is trying to tell you that he or she is not satisfied with the relationship. Your mate may feel threatened, distant, fearful, sad, lonely, or any combination of these things. One doesn't know how to say that he or she wants to get closer. It all comes out as complaint, criticism, and/or anger.

So what should you say to a partner when you're angry or feel threats? Tell him or her what you *really* feel.

There is More than Anger

Anger is called a "secondary emotion." That means that anger rarely is present by itself. Other emotions are present and precede the anger. These usually include: anxiety, guilt and/or hurt.

These emotions are not pleasant. Most people would rather avoid feeling them. So our automatic response kicks in: get angry and complain. Most of the time it's so automatic that people aren't even aware of their other emotions. Getting angry is not only easier, it has the added bonus of laying some guilt and blame on someone.

This may be hard to believe, but it's true. I have seen many people for couples counseling. Without exception, partners learn to identify the other emotions behind their anger.

If you're the pursuer/complainer, try to say clearly what you feel. Try to state your other emotions. Try to say that there is a threat or a difficulty with the relationship. More on how to do this is covered in the next chapter.

If you're the recipient of the complaints, remember that many feelings are being left out. Your partner is often feeling hurt or anxious. Secondly, remember that your partner is worried about the relationship. Thirdly, your partner is trying to get closer through the complaining. So try to listen for the real message. Lastly, resist defending yourself or withdrawing. Share your other feelings, not just your irritation.

He Won't Talk to Me

John would drive Pat crazy. She would complain or ask him about something he was involved with. Most of the time, he would angrily defend himself. Sometimes he would just throw his hands up in the air and give in, grudgingly.

Pat could not understand why he reacted this way. Things got so bad that she was afraid to say anything to him. She could hold it in only so long. Then her anger would be triggered and their Dance would begin.

John, the Defender, took Pat's complaining personally. Always. Whenever she complained or was angry about anything, he felt criticized.

Now John deeply loved his wife. When he heard her complain, it was like a knife in his heart. He badly wanted her love and praise. He could not tolerate the idea that she did not love him. Any complaint suggested that she was criticizing him and regretting her love. So he automatically, without thinking, defended himself. It was his way of trying to persuade her to see that he was an OK and loveable guy.

Sometimes John could not take another fight, so he would just give in. Other times he ignored her because his emotions were too powerful and overwhelming. John could not distinguish between different kinds of complaints. He was programmed to see all complaints as statements of his deficiency as a husband. He went into the relationship with the dangerous assumption that all of Pat's complaints were directed at him. No wonder he reacted as he did.

It's important to question your assumptions. Your partner's complaints may not have anything to do with what you think. Instead of reacting, try to do two things. One, ask you partner questions. Find out if he or she really is criticizing or complaining about you. Secondly, remember that anger is a secondary emotion. Try to express the other things you're feeling.

Hot Buttons

In the Dance, your "hot button" is always pushed. Whenever Pat complained, John, without thinking, automatically reacted. This is *the* big clue that his hot button got pushed.

Jeff also reacted whenever his wife, Tina, disagreed with him. He became angry, often yelling at her. This was his Hot Button: Tina disagreeing with him. But what did it mean for him?

After a few sessions Jeff was able to figure it out. Whenever his wife told him that she disagreed with him, he thought she was rejecting him. He could not stand the idea that she was rejecting him. So he angrily reacted, trying to convince her to agree with him.

Notice that Jeff's Hot Button involves his partner's beliefs and attitudes about him. Actually, it's more accurate to say that it involves what Jeff thinks his wife believes about him. If Tina disagrees, Jeff interprets it to mean that she is rebuffing him. It doesn't matter whether or not his wife is actually doing this. It's all about how Jeff interprets her attitude toward him. This is a major piece of hot buttons.

But wait, there's more! The hot button is also powered by your attitude toward yourself. This is harder to understand and see.

Jeff reacts. When somebody touches his sensitive hot button, he gets upset. So there must be something in him that causes this reaction. We already know that he becomes angry when his wife disagrees, because it means she rejects him. But why is this so? What else is happening inside of Jeff?

Let's imagine I upgraded my living room with new floors and trim. Since I have completed a good deal of work like this in the past, I do a great job with the project. My know-it-all friend visits and states that I made several mistakes. I know that I have done a "good job" so I ignore him and let it go. What he says doesn't bother me.

But what if I wasn't so sure about myself? Let's say I doubted my abilities. Suppose I was unsure not only about the quality of my work but also about my abilities as a finish carpenter? How might I then react? In the past, I reacted with defensive anger. I can't really tell my friend about my doubts about myself. It's too disturbing for me to even contemplate. My doubts about myself are real, but unexpressed. So what do I do about these emotions? I express them through anger. I get angrily defensive with my friend. Sound familiar?

In the second scenario, my friend triggers my hot button and I react. I think he is criticizing me through my work. But the "doubts" about me power my reactions. These doubts reveal my self-image. Simply, I do not believe that I am adequate. This is the basic pattern or template we experience with hot buttons. We see ourselves as inadequate, as failures, as unworthy or faulty in some way. We fear that this is true and try to keep this little secret to ourselves. So when someone inadvertently points out our deficiency and reveals our secret, we react defensively and angrily. Our hot button gains power from our doubts about ourselves.

Getting back to Jeff, most of the time he thought he was an OK guy. But there was a part of him that did not believe this. A part of him feared he was often not right. This part knew how many mistakes he made and how worthless he was. He secretly believed that he was a failure.

It was as if Jeff had two parts. One piece believed he was an OK guy. But another piece believed he was a mistake-prone failure. So when Tina disagreed with him, this second part was activated. It tried to defend Jeff by becoming angry. Jeff is not alone. Most of us have deep-seated doubts about ourselves. These are the painful beliefs that underlay our hot buttons. Like most people, these beliefs are only part of what makes Jeff who he is. In other ways, he felt confident and secure. But sometimes, in situations with his attachment love, these insecurities came out.

Most of us have some kind of Hot Button, some kind of hy-persensitivity. It's rooted in that part of us that truly believes the worst in us. It all has to do with what we believe about ourselves.

It works this way.

1. We have a belief, opinion, attitude about ourselves.
2. This attitude puts us in a bad light.
3. We fear it's true.

4. So we try to hide it.

5. When our attachment lover seems to say that this belief is true, we react.

6. Sometimes we rip his or her head off.

7. Sometimes we withdraw (depending on our attachment style).

8. Your lover probably has no idea what happened.

Jeff ended up taking a risk and admitting to Tina that he had these serious doubts about himself. He was surprised and happy to discover that Tina loved him anyway.

In this chapter, a number of important ideas were presented:

1. It's important for both couples to accept responsibility for the problems in the relationship.

2. The real problem is the Dance, which stops communication and creates anger.

3. Blaming your partner can lead to contempt, which kills relationships.

4. Sometimes people fear being dependent on their partners.

5. Problem-solving tendencies can get in the way of closeness.

6. For relationships to succeed, couples must listen and communicate emotionally to each other.

7. Pursuers who complain are only trying to re-establish closeness.

8. Anger is a secondary emotion. Other emotions are always present with it. Share these other emotions with your partner.

9. Ask your partner for clarification. Your interpretation might be wrong.

10. Hot buttons trigger the Dance.

11. Hot buttons always touch a part of our self-image which we dislike, hate, or want to forget.

Chapter 13

figuring out your dance

❧

This chapter gives you concrete ways of getting closer to your mate. You will find exercises designed to help you better identify your dance.

The exercises include:

- ♥ Focusing on emotions.
- ♥ Learning how to Focus.
- ♥ Identifying significant arguments.
- ♥ Identifying your dance.
- ♥ Identifying your partner's dance.

Emotions

Emotions are key to building closeness to your partner.

When these emotions are authentically expressed and responded to, understanding and intimacy emerge.

There are not really a great many emotions. Psychologists argue about how many basic emotions exist. I go with the following:

♥ Anger   ♥ Hurt

♥ Sadness   ♥ Shame or guilt

♥ Anxiety   ♥ Surprise

♥ Happiness   ♥ Disgust

If you want to add or subtract a few, go ahead. I won't argue with you. All the other words for emotions are just variations of a few basic ones.

Focus on Emotions

Many people simply don't focus on their emotions. They observe their physical sensations and thoughts, but they have not trained themselves to focus on anything else.

The process is simplicity itself. It's different than solving a problem. In a problem, one thinks about the issues and figures out a solution. It's a cognitive, thinking process. With emotions, you do not try to figure out what you're feeling. You try to *discover* what is there, by looking and observing. You discover what emotion you feel by uncovering it.

Simply concentrate on something. Then look to see what emotions accompany it. As an example, imagine yourself running away from a bear. What emotions accompany the image? When you image that you're on a beach by the ocean, what emotions accompany the image?

You can also gaze at a picture. Then look to see what emotions you experience.

Many times, you may find that you have more than one emotion. So it's important to go through the whole list.

Identifying emotions is not magical. It's just a skill. The more you practice, the better you get at it.

Identifying Arguments

Make a list of arguments with your partner. Concentrate on ones which caused a fight. Two conditions have to be met:

1. Concentrate on the ones that resulted from your anger or dissatisfaction.

2. These situations must involve your being hurt, feeling threatened, or your feeling that the relationship was damaged in some way.

It could be a time when your partner insulted you, let you down, or slighted you. It has to be something you see as a threat to the relationship.

Now, do the exercise from your partner's point of view. Make a list of arguments that your partner started. Write down the precipitating events or statements. Look for any patterns.

Identifying My Half of the Dance

Remember, your Dance is *the* central obstacle to your relationship. Once in it, couples trigger each other's hot button and trip all over each other. They don't listen to each other. They argue. They end up feeling resentful and distant from each other. In general, one partner is the pursuer/complainer; the other plays the role of withdrawer/defender. Sometimes both partners are pursuers or defenders, though this is relatively rare.

It's important to recognize your basic Dance pattern. If you don't know what you are doing, how can you change it? Take one of the specific situations from the previous exercise. Use one in which you became angry at your partner.

Ask yourself what you did or said when you were upset. Write down how your partner would respond. Identify how you responded or what you did. What did your partner say or do next? How did the argument end? When did you make up? Who made the first move to make up? Write all of this down. Now re-do the above exercise two or three more times. But use different arguments.

Try to identify the pattern. Re-read the chapters on The Dance. Do you fall into one of the categories?

Do you tend to complain when he won't respond to you? This is one trait of a pursuer.

Do you feel hurt and defend yourself when he complains? This is one trait of a withdrawer.

Remember, look for general patterns of behavior. I do this; he does that. I do something else; he ends up doing something really dumb that drives me nuts!

Identifying My Partner's Half of the Dance

Now look at your patterns from another perspective. From the exercise above, identify one of the conflict situations which gets your partner going.

Again, ask yourself what your partner did or said when he or she was upset. How did you respond? Identify what your partner said or did next. What did you say or do next? How did the argument end? When did you make up? Who made the first move to make up? Write all of this down. Now re-do the above exercise two or three more times. But use different situations.

Look for patterns of responses. Re-read the chapters on The Dance. Now you may be able to write down a more detailed description of your pattern. It should include what both of you do. It should also include a statement of your attachment style and your partner's (either pursuer or withdrawer).

Now here comes a tricky part. Some people may find that they may have more than one Dance. So they may respond somewhat differently in different situations. Or they may respond in more complex ways. For example, the pursuer may try hard for several years to get a spouse to emotionally engage with them. But they often get tired and give up at some point. They stop pursuing and become a withdrawer.

I know of one couple in which the woman is the pursuer. Her partner tends to defend himself or withdraw. But when he becomes angry, she gets triggered into a complete withdrawal (she can't stand his anger).

So your Dance may be more complex than some other ones. This is OK. It just makes your job a little harder.

I also notice that people have a predominate style. But they may adopt another style in different situations. For example, a male withdrawer, who never complains, suddenly criticizes his wife. She starts defending herself. Often, in therapy, I see this.

The Dance can be straightforward or it can be more complex. In either event, write down your Dance. Don't worry about getting it absolutely, perfectly right. This is not an exam. Get it down as best you can.

OK, Now What?

First, share the information with your partner. Ask for feedback and his or her perspective on things. Be gentle. The purpose is not to blame your mate for the Dance. The idea is to see that it's your Dance which keeps you from being close. The first way to do something is to talk about it and how it keeps you apart.

Second, start noticing when you are entering the Dance. Change doesn't happen overnight. Try to catch yourself when you get in the dance. Stop and ask each other: are we doing it? Third, turn to the next chapter and begin some exercises there. The heart of the Dance is your pushing each other's hot buttons. It's important to start identifying what triggers you and your partner.

Chapter 14

hot buttons

~·ᖰᖰᖱᖱ·~

Acouple will be talking or playing. All of a sudden, in a flash, they are in a life-and-death argument. Their Dance captured them.

What happened?

Partner A said or did something. This touched a sensitive button in Partner B. B automatically reacted with anger. This anger touched a sensitive button in Partner A. A then automatically reacted. The Dance is on.

Once you know your Dance pattern, the hot buttons come next. The hot buttons is just a way to initiate our automatic, non-thinking reaction. But you have to know it before you can do anything about it.

The Trigger

Write down one of the precipitating events of an argument. Just take one that you have from the previous chapter. Again, focus on it. Try to re-live it in your mind, as though you were going through it at this moment.

Write down, on the left side of the paper, the feelings you have about that situation. Next to the feelings, write down the thoughts connected to your feelings. So, I might feel angry because he calls me a name. I feel sad because I want him to like me. I feel hurt because he doesn't like me.

This is a good start. But you have to dig a little deeper. The Dance and the hot buttons all have to do with your relationship. They are connected to how your partner sees you.

When our love appears threatened in some way, we react. An event or words trigger something in us. The trigger is always about how you see your partner *and* how your partner sees you.

Let me give you some examples. A few chapters ago, I noted that my client was angry because her husband called her a name. She also realized that she felt hurt by what he said. I pushed her to tell us what thoughts were connected with her hurt. She said that she felt hurt because he thought she was stupid.

This was a threat to her attachment love. She wanted to be close to her husband. He called that into question when he called her a name. How could he love someone who was stupid? She reacted angrily, felt hurt and thought he saw her as being ignorant or dumb.

The truth has to do with *how your partner sees you*. More accurately, the feeling and meaning have to do with how you *think* your partner sees you. My client above felt hurt because her husband thought or acted as though she was a dummy. She felt hurt because he did not respect her. She reacted in anger.

In the major fights of the Dance, this is always the case. Your feelings are connected with what you believe your partner is saying about you. These are not pleasant thoughts. Otherwise you would not get angry.

Go back to the beginning of this section and review what you wrote down.

On the right side of the page, next to the feelings and thoughts, write down how your attachment love is threatened. Try to be as specific as possible. This is key to the exercise.

It may take some time for you to uncover your feelings. It may take more effort to connect those feelings with your thoughts. That is OK. Everybody proceeds at his or her own pace. But believe me, there is more there than just anger.

Split Up

Sometimes people ignore their own answers. They focus on that tense moment, identify that hurt, connect a meaning to it and then blow it off. You say to yourself, "I know that she doesn't really think like this. So I must be wrong."

No, you are not wrong. It's as if we are of two minds. There is a part of us that may see our partner in one light. But another part of us reacts in a different way. It's like you are split up. Different parts of you react differently.

You may very well know that your partner loves you. But at that moment, when you are triggered in the Dance, there is another part of you that reacts. This is your hot button.

In fact, anytime you automatically react with anger your hot button has been touched. Your partner says or does something; you give it a negative meaning and you react. It happens so quickly, doesn't it?

You have identified above what triggers you. Now you have to figure out what it says about you. Usually it's some kind of secret fear you have about yourself. Hot buttons have to do with your self-image. This powers your automatic reactions in your Dance.

We already know that you automatically react to something your partner says. But what in you is reacting? What is being triggered? What in you is lashing out?

Take the results of your exercise above. Ask yourself: what does my reaction say about me? What does it say about what I believe about myself? What does it say that I fear about myself?

Figuring out the belief is direct. Look at what your partner is saying or doing. This is the trigger. If it touches your hot button, you must believe there is some truth to it. Otherwise you would stay calm.

Since this is a difficult exercise, let me give you an example.

> *Al was a defender. When his wife, Sue, complained, he got angry and defended himself. Eventually, he was able to state that he hated her complaints. He believed it was his fault. He felt unloved. He thought Sue was telling him he was inadequate because he failed her.*
>
> *His trigger was her criticism. His response was deep shame that he failed (he had a hard time admitting this).*
>
> *This is the clue. You have to ask yourself: why would someone react so dramatically to any suggestion of failure? Why hide his shame of failure?*
>
> *He believed that he had to be perfect, that he always had to succeed. His deep down fear was that he truly was a failure. Any suggestion of failure triggered his anger and defensive attack on his wife. This was Al's part of the dance. This was his hot button.*

When you are finished with the exercise, you should have a good idea of your Hot Button and what it means for you.

Now do the exercise with your partner in mind.

Beginning a New Dance

Suppose you use the pursuer style. When upset about some harm to the relationship, you react by complaining. You may even angrily criticize your partner.

But you are not really being totally honest with your partner. In the exercise from the previous chapter, a lot more feelings came out. Yet you only tell your partner one thing: irritation and complaints. So tell him more. Share with him your feelings: all of them. Share your sadness, hurt, fears, whatever you uncovered. It's OK to say you are irritated. But also share the rest of it. Tell about how you were triggered because you thought there was a threat.

When you express to your significant other your feelings and thoughts, try not to accuse. Believe it or not, your partner probably loves you. Yet he or she may not realize what you are reacting to. Your partner may not know how to respond. So go easy.

If you are a withdrawer, resist the temptation to defend yourself. If you have completed some of the exercises above, you know that you have a lot more feelings. So tell your partner more about what is going on inside of you.

Explain how difficult it is to share or how you feel awkward, embarrassed or afraid and vulnerable. Tell him or her what you have uncovered in your work. Using the information from the above exercises, take a risk and open up, at least a little.

Eventually, after some trust is built up, tell your partner about your hot button and about the fears that drive it.

Take Your Time

Now, be realistic. To do this kind of work is frightening. It entails a risk that your partner might not care or might even reject you. So take your time with it. Test the waters. You don't have to share everything all at once. Ease into this new phase of your relationship, giving your partner time to change.

Don't worry if you and your partner still get caught up in your Dance. Adjusting your communications with each other and avoiding the Dance doesn't occur overnight. Most people follow a gradual process. First one becomes aware of the pattern and commits to change. Then one does his or her Dance, but only realizes this after the fight is over. Eventually each starts to catch oneself in the middle of the Dance. Following this, the partners begin avoiding the Dance altogether. Give yourselves time and understanding.

Sometimes, partners are caught unawares of new behavior. Then they do not know how to interpret the emotional sharing. After all, we all get into habits. Being accustomed to particular behavior your partner will expect certain reactions. When something different occurs, your mate may not believe it.

Jim heard his wife share her fears, instead of criticizing him. He didn't believe her. He thought she was trying to manipulate him. He heard it but misinterpreted her feelings. He did not understand that she wanted to change the Dance.

So don't give up. Give your partner time to take in the new information. Keep at it over a period of weeks or longer. Most of the time, it will eventually seep in.

Sharing and Trust

All of these exercises lead to one thing: sharing. Sharing our feelings and vulnerabilities leads to closeness, intimacy, and the sure knowledge that your partner is someone you can trust.

epilogue

Intimate relationships are based upon attachment love. Even though most Westerners marry because they have fallen-in-love, much more is necessary for a marriage, or any intimate relationship, to succeed. Falling-in-love is not enough.

In this book, I have introduced you to the principles of attachment love, how it plays out in relationships, how our hot buttons can distort our love, and some ways to improve.

As I noted, it's not easy to change our old patterns. There is no magic pill that will automatically make it all better. But you can improve your relationship. It can be done with work, effort, and commitment.

I wish you the best in your intimate relationships.

For more information, see the resource list and look up: www.keepinglove.com.

resources

Alberoni (1983). *Falling in Love*. Westminster, Maryland: Random House, Inc.

Arp, D., and Arp, C. (1997). *10 Great Dates to Energize Your Marriage*. Grand Rapids, Mich.: Zondervan.

Arp, D., and Arp, C. (1998). *Love Life for Parents*. Grand Rapids, Mich.: Zondervan.

Arterburn, S., Stoeker, F, and Yorkev, M. (2000). *Every Man's Marriage: An Every Man's Guide to Winning the Heart of a Woman*.

Baron, R. and Wagele E. (1995). *Are You My Type, am I Yours?* San Francisco: Harper San Francisco.

Bowlby, J. (1988). *A Secure Base*. New York: Basic.

Chapman, G. (2004). *The Five Love Languages: How to Express Heartfelt Commitment to Your Mate*. Grand Rapids, MI: Zondervan

Christensen, A., and Jacobson, N. S. (2000). *Reconcilable Differences*. New York: Guilford.

Clifford, N., and Clifford, C. I. (1994). *We Can Work It Out: How to Solve Conflicts, Save Your Marriage, and Strengthen Your Love for Each Other*. New York: The Berkley Publishing Group.

Cloud, H., and Townsend, J. (1999). *Boundaries in Marriage*. Grand Rapids, MI: Zondervan.

Dragun, J. (2007). *Couples Workbook on Attachment Love*. Brighton, MI: Canton Press

Dyer, W. (1999). *Your Erroneous Zones*. New York: HarperCollins.

Fisher, H. (2004). *Why We Love: The Nature and Chemistry of Romantic Love.* New York: Henry Holt and Company, LLC.

Glass, S., and Staeheli, J. (2003). *Not "Just Friends": Rebuilding Trust and Recovering Your Sanity After Infidelity.* New York: Free Press.

Gottman, J., and N. Silver. (1999) *The Seven Principles for Making Marriage Work.* New York: Three Rivers Press.

Gray, J. (1992). *Men are from Mars, Women are from Venus.* New York: Harper Collins.

Johnson, S., Makinen, J. and Millikin, J. (2001). Attachment injuries in couple relationships: a new perspective on impasses in couples therapy. Journal of Marital and Family Therapy, April, 2001, Vol. 27, No. 2, 145-155.

Markman, H., Stanley, S., and Blumberg, S. L. (1994). *Fighting for Your Marriage.* San Ellico: Jossey-Bass.

Murphy, Francis, Ed. (1996). *Walt Whitman: The Complete Poems.* London, England: Penguin Books, Ltd.

Parrott, L., and Parrott, L. (1995). *Saving your Marriage Before it Starts: Seven Questions to Ask Before (and After) You Marry.* Grand Rapids, MI: Zondervan.

Smalley J. and Trent, J. (1995). *The Language of Love.* New York: Pocket Books.

Spring, J. (1997). *After the Affair: Healing the Pain and Rebuilding Trust When a Partner Has Been Unfaithful.*

Thomas, G. (1999). *Sacred Marriage.* Grand Rapids, MI: Zondervan

Toner, Jules (1969) *What is Love?* Washington, D.C.: Corpus Books.

Wallerstein, J.S., And Blakeslee, S. (1996). *The Good Marriage: How and Why Love Lasts.* New York: Warner Books.

Web Resources

Alliance for Marriage
www.allianceformarriages.com

BellaOnline
www.bellaonline.com/channel/c12.asp

eNotAlone: resources on abuse
www.enotalone.com/92-1.html

Marriage Encounter
www.wme.org

National Marriage Project
http://marriage.rutgers.edu

Psychology Today
www.psychologtoday.com/topics/relationships.html

Smart Marriages
www.smartmarriages.com

index